The Foreign and Security Policy of the European Union

Past, Present and Future

Fraser Cameron

★ UACES ★

Sheffield
Academic Press

Copyright © 1999 Sheffield Academic Press

Published by
Sheffield Academic Press Ltd
Mansion House
19 Kingfield Road
Sheffield S11 9AS
England

Typeset by Sheffield Academic Press
and
Printed on acid-free paper in Great Britain
by Cromwell Press
Trowbridge, Wiltshire

British Library Cataloguing in Publication Data

A catalogue record for this book is available
from the British Library

ISBN 1-84127-001-6

Contents

Tables

Figures

Foreword

There is a growing public consensus that the European Union should be more effective in foreign and security policy. The tragedy of the events in former Yugoslavia, especially Bosnia and Kosovo, and the continuing instability in Europe's periphery demonstrate the need for a stronger, more coherent and consistent approach to external relations.

The European Commission has consistently pushed for such an approach but in the past there has been a failure of political will among the Member States to act together. Now there is a fresh opportunity to move forward. With the entry into force of the Treaty of Amsterdam and its new, strengthened provisions for the CFSP, plus the changed British attitude towards European defence, the time is right for the European Union to demonstrate that it has the capacity and will to act in foreign and security policy.

In doing so the EU would be responding to the wishes of its citizens and principal partners. With 370 million people, with a GDP equal to that of the United States, with the largest single market in the world, as the most important player in international trade, as the main source of development assistance and humanitarian aid, the EU cannot avoid taking increased responsibility in world affairs.

I, therefore, welcome this book which explains the origins of the CFSP, analyses its current operation and offers some interesting ideas for its future development. It deserves a wide readership.

Neil Kinnock
Vice President,
European Commission

Series Foreword

This is the seventh publication in the series Contemporary European Studies which represents a continuing collaboration between the University Association for Contemporary European Studies (UACES) and Sheffield Academic Press.

UACES, the foremost British organization that brings together academics and practitioners concerned with the study of contemporary Europe, celebrates its thirtieth anniversary in 2000. The main emphasis of the Association's work has been in the field of European integration, in particular on the institutions and policies of the European Union. This series aims at reflecting these interests by meeting the needs of those studying and teaching about contemporary Europe by providing authoritative texts dealing with a wide range of issues, with the emphasis on the European Union.

The European Union has become increasingly engaged in its Common Foreign and Security Policy (CFSP) since its establishment by the Maastricht Treaty in 1992. The policy has involved a complex of institutions and actors in the international field. This book provides the background to and an evaluation of the CFSP and also examines the developments brought to the policy by the Treaty of Amsterdam of 1997. The author, Fraser Cameron, until September 1999, served with the directorate of the European Commission dealing with EU enlargement and with the Central and East European states, and, since then, has been part of the Commission's Delegation in Washington, DC. His contribution on this subject is thus both timely and authoritative.

In the production of this book I am grateful to Neil Kinnock of the European Commission, for kindly providing a Foreword, and to Jean Allen and Rebecca Cullen and the staff at Sheffield Academic Press for their assistance.

Clive Archer
Series Editor

Acknowledgments

As with the previous book in this series I would like to thank Solveig Jaspert for all her efforts in ensuring the manuscript saw the light of day, and Clive Archer and Rebecca Cullen for their editorial comments.

The opinions expressed are of course personal and do not commit the European Commission in any way.

Abbreviations

ACP	African, Caribbean and Pacific
APEC	Asia Pacific Economic Co-operation
ASEAN	Association of Southeast Asian Nations
BSCC	Baltic Sea Co-operation Council
BSEC	Black Sea Economic Co-operation
CEEC	Central and Eastern European Countries
CEFTA	Central European Free Trade Area
CFSP	Common Foreign and Security Policy
CIS	Commonwealth of Independent States
CJTF	Combined Joint Task Forces
CPN	Conflict Prevention Network
CSCE	Conference on Security and Cooperation in Europe
EAPC	Euro Atlantic Partnership Council
EBRD	European Bank for Reconstruction and Development
EC	European Community
ECHO	European Community Humanitarian Organization
ECMM	European Community Monitoring Mission
ECSC	European Coal and Steel Community
EDC	European Defence Community
EEA	European Economic Area
EEC	European Economic Community
EFTA	European Free Trade Association
EIB	European Investment Bank
EMU	Economic and Monetary Union
EP	European Parliament
EPC	European Political Cooperation
ESDI	European Security and Defence Identity
EU	European Union
EUAM	European Union Administration of Mostar
FAO	Food and Agricultural Organization
FRY	Federal Republic of Yugoslavia
FYROM	Former Yugoslav Republic of Macedonia
GAC	General Affairs Council
GATT	General Agreement on Trade and Tariffs

GSP	generalized system of preference
IGC	Intergovernmental Conference
MEPP	Middle East Peace Process
MoU	Memorandum of Understanding
NAFTA	North American Free Trade Agreement
NATO	North Atlantic Treaty Organization
NGO	non-government organization
NIS	Newly Independent States
NPT	Non Proliferation Treaty
OECD	Organization for Economic Cooperation and Development
OSCE	Organization for Security and Co-operation in Europe
PCA	Partnership and Co-operation Agreement
PfP	Partnership for Peace
PHARE	Poland,Hungary (Assistance for Economic Reconstruction)
QMV	qualified majority voting
SEA	Single European Act
TACIS	Technical Assistance to Commonwealth of Independent States
TEU	Treaty on European Union
UN	United Nations
UNSC	United Nations Security Council
WEU	Western European Union
WTO	World Trade Organization

Introduction

The idea for this book arose when the author (together with Graham Avery) had completed the first book in the UACES series, *The Enlargement of the European Union*. There were a growing number of books covering aspects of the European Union's common foreign and security policy (CFSP), but no guide explaining the origins of CFSP, how it worked in practice, let alone offering some ideas for the future.

Europe: The Strange Superpower, *The Paradoxes of European Foreign Policy*, *From Civilian Power to Superpower?* and *Europe: The Ambiguous Power* are just a few of the recent books on the Union's external relations which reflect the difficulty of analysing the EU's foreign and security policy. The EU has steadily grown as an actor in international affairs but its power and influence are predominantly in the domain of 'soft security'.[1] It has important political, economic, trade and financial instruments but it still has not developed a credible military capability to support its diplomacy. There are, however, encouraging signs that this may be changing. The turnaround in British attitudes towards European defence and the changed views in Germany and France have led to a larger convergence on security issues than was conceivable just a few years ago.

However, it is one thing to agree that something should be done to improve the EU's ability to act and another to achieve a consensus on exactly what should be done and to ensure that it is done. On the eve of a new millennium Europeans have important choices to make as to what kind of Union they wish to have and what role this Union should play on the world stage.

Given the modest beginnings of cooperation in the sensitive field of foreign and security policy, it is perhaps worth asking the question

---

1.   The term 'soft security' refers to non-military aspects of security. It usually includes political, economic, financial, trade and environmental issues as well as 'third pillar' concerns such as illegal immigration and cross-border crime.

whether the EU still needs a CFSP. The answer is 'yes' for a number of reasons. First, the voice of Europe will only be heard in world affairs if there is a single voice, otherwise it will not be heard at all. Secondly, the end of the Cold War has dramatically changed the European Union's strategic situation. The Soviet threat has disappeared, but many different new risks have appeared. They are risks that need to be handled collectively by the Union otherwise they cannot be handled in an effective manner. Thirdly, the United States has reduced its military presence in Europe and pressed the EU to take on more responsibility for its own security and regional security.

The first chapter considers the ideas of the Founding Fathers of European integration on security issues, reviews the proposals for a European Defence Community (EDC) in the 1950s and discusses the creation and operation of the system of European Political Cooperation (EPC). The second chapter covers the establishment of the CFSP, analyses the debates during the negotiations leading to the Treaty of Maastricht and includes an assessment of the EU's performance in dealing with the Yugoslav crisis. The third chapter describes CFSP structures, while the fourth chapter examines the CFSP in operation including a review of three of the first joint actions—the Stability Pact, the administration of Mostar and the lobbying for an extension of the Non-Proliferation Treaty (NPT). The changes made as a result of the Treaty of Amsterdam are reviewed in Chapter 5, and Chapter 6 considers the security and defence dimension of the CFSP. Chapter 7 then sets the CFSP against the positive balance sheet of the EU's overall external relations. Chapter 8 examines the challenges facing the CFSP and Chapter 9 concludes by looking towards the future.

There is a sizeable bibliography, including many useful website addresses, and a number of appendixes containing treaty and other documentary extracts.

Fraser Cameron

1 |

Life before the CFSP

The Founding Fathers of the European Union[1] (or European Communities in the 1950s) always considered that there should be a security dimension to their unique undertaking. Their thinking was motivated by the three catastrophic wars which had been fought in Europe between 1871 and 1945, all involving Germany and France fighting each other. By the end of the Second World War it was clear that the United States and the Soviet Union would play the dominant role in European security. London, Paris and Rome had lost influence while Berlin was divided between the major powers. The Founding Fathers understood that the European states could only regain international influence by working together. Their idea for a supra-national European Community in which states would share their sovereignty was thus a major contribution to creating a genuine security community between the participating states.

The first sectors chosen for integration were the coal and steel industries with their huge symbolic importance as the industries that had fuelled the war machines on both sides. France, West Germany, Italy, Belgium, Luxembourg and the Netherlands (but not the UK) formed the European Coal and Steel Community (ECSC) in 1951. The Treaty of Paris establishing the ECSC defined its creation in the preamble as a contribution to the safeguarding of world peace. After the successful establishment of the ECSC, the visionaries of the early 1950s turned their attention to political and defence integration. The French proposed to establish a European army within a European Defence Community (EDC) which would come under the political authority of a European Political Community (EPC).

1. The Founding Fathers is the name given to statesmen such as Robert Schuman, Konrad Adenauer and Jean Monnet who translated vision into political reality. One of the best books analysing this period is Richard Mayne (1969). For a closer examination of the term 'security community' see the writings of Karl Deutsch (1957).

This proposal was widely welcomed among the six founding members of the ECSC, particularly by West Germany who saw it as offering a swift path back to international acceptability. But the plan failed at the final hurdle—ironically ratification in the French Senate owing to concerns about the supra-national aspects of the EDC. The proposals for defence and political integration were thus shelved. West Germany became a member of NATO and also joined the Western European Union (WEU), a defence alliance which had been established between the UK, France, Italy and the Benelux countries in 1948.

But the idea for closer cooperation in this sensitive area did not disappear. After the creation of the European Economic Community (EEC) in 1957 the French relaunched their proposals for political and defence cooperation with the Fouchet Plan in 1961 (Bloes 1970). President de Gaulle's motive in doing so was to increase French influence by operating and leading a wider grouping which could provide more of a counterweight than France alone to the two superpowers. The French plans called for a Union of European Peoples which would have a common foreign and defence policy as well as political, economic and cultural cooperation. The Union would be based on an intergovernmental system with fixed financial contributions.

In many ways the Fouchet Plan (named after the French diplomat and de Gaulle confidante leading the negotiations) was the forerunner of the CFSP. But it did not get off the ground in 1962 because of opposition from the Netherlands and Belgium at the exclusion of Britain and doubts in Bonn and Rome at the anti-US tone of de Gaulle's rhetoric. The French President despaired of Britain playing a part in European defence after Prime Minister Macmillan signed a nuclear missile deal with the US at Nassau in 1962 and used this as an argument to veto the UK's entry into the EEC in January 1963 (de Gaulle 1971). Although the Fouchet Plan failed it led to a discussion of the many sensitive security issues in Europe and was a guide for later attempts at cooperation.

In 1969 President de Gaulle resigned paving the way for new efforts to promote European integration. The six founding members, anticipating the future membership of Britain, Denmark and Ireland, issued a declaration at the 1969 Hague Summit which called for 'a united Europe capable of assuming its responsibilities in the world of tomorrow and of making a contribution commensurate with its tradition and mission'. The summit agreed to establish a committee of senior officials to prepare a report on political cooperation.

The subsequent report, known sometimes as the Davignon report, after the chairman of the committee, was adopted by the foreign ministers meeting in the Luxembourg report. The report stated the EU's aims as being 'to move towards political unification' and as a necessary step it was proposed to establish a system of European Political Co-operation (EPC).[2] This was a determined effort to increase the weight of the EC in international affairs by providing for the regular exchange of information and meetings of foreign ministers and senior officials to cooperate and coordinate foreign policy positions and actions. Although with de Gaulle's departure the EC had lost the strongest opponent of the community method of doing business, the French still insisted on establishing the EPC on intergovernmental lines outside EC structures.[3] As a symbol of the difference in EPC operating procedures, meetings were to be held in the capital of the rotating Presidency and not in Brussels. This debate on how to operate foreign and security policy was to re-emerge two decades later during the Maastricht Treaty negotiations.

Most EPC business was transacted by the Political Committee (composed of Political Directors in foreign ministries and the Commission) aided by a group of junior officials (European Correspondents) who handled routine business. There were just two languages used (English and French) without interpretation. A secure telegraphic network (Coreu) was also established to facilitate communications between partners. The public, however, was largely unaware of these changes. As a former practitioner has argued, EPC was akin to 'a private club, operated by diplomats, for diplomats' (Nuttall 1992: 11).

In the early years of EPC there was some success in coordinating the positions of Member States on subjects such as the Middle East and the Conference on Security and Cooperation in Europe (CSCE) (Cameron 1995). The Commission and Member States worked closely in the negotiations leading up to the Helsinki Final Act of 1975. This led to a steadily increasing EC profile in international affairs, even if the EC could hardly be described as a decisive player. Its response to the Soviet invasion of Afghanistan on 26 December 1979 showed how

---

2.   The most comprehensive work on the EPC is that by Simon Nuttall (1992). See also Hill (1983).

3.   The 'community method' refers to the Commission's sole right of initiative with most decisions taken by qualified majority vote in the Council after consultation with the European Parliament.

difficult it was for the EPC to react to a fast-moving crisis. In 1981 some improvements, outlined in the London report, were made to the EPC, including the creation of a troika (the present holder of the rotating EC Presidency together with the immediate past and future members and the Commission) to assist the Presidency in representing the EC, and provision for cooperation between Member States in third countries and at international organizations. A series of working groups was also established to prepare reports for decision by the Political Committee.[4]

During the 1980s the EC also began to link its external relations transacted under the traditional Community method to those under the EPC. Examples include the imposition of economic sanctions on the Soviet Union after the 1981 declaration of martial law in Poland; on Argentine after the invasion of the Falklands in 1982; on the apartheid régime in South Africa; and on Saddam Hussein's government following the Iraqi invasion of Kuwait. However, defence remained a taboo area and there was no coordinated European response to a number of military questions such as the acceptance of US cruise and Pershing missiles in Europe in the early 1980s. The United States, particularly the Reagan administration, was at once concerned at some of the policy stances taken under EPC (for example, those opposed to US policy in Central America and Libya) and critical of the alleged EC failure to combat international terrorism.

In 1987 EPC was given a treaty base, Article 30 of the Single European Act (SEA), which codified the procedures that had been established since 1970 and created a secretariat in Brussels that could assist the Presidency and provide for better preparation of meetings and greater continuity.

Under the treaty, the members undertook 'to inform and consult each other on any foreign policy matters of general interest so as to ensure that their combined influence is exercised as effectively as possible through co-ordination, the convergence of their positions and implementation of joint action'. These consultations were to take place before the parties decided on their final position. Common principles and objectives were to be gradually developed and defined and in order to ensure the swift adoption and implementation of common or joint actions. The parties were, as far as possible, 'to refrain from impeding the formation of a consensus'. The EPC could discuss the 'political and

---

4.   See the Glossary for an explanation of the institutions.

economic aspects of security' but military issues remained out of bounds. The European Parliament was to be regularly informed about the EPC and its views taken into consideration. There was a bow in the direction of consistency of external action with the Presidency and the Commission charged with the responsibility 'for ensuring that such consistency is sought and maintained'. Further provisions touched on cooperation in international organizations and arrangements for political dialogue with third countries.

The principal arrangements were as follows:

Article XXX of the Single European Act (1987) establishing European Political Co-operation

European co-operation in the sphere of Foreign Policy shall be governed by the following provisions:

1.   The High Contracting Parties, being members of the European Communities, shall endeavour jointly to formulate and implement a European Foreign Policy.

2. a) The High Contracting Parties undertake to inform and consult each other on any Foreign Policy Matters of general interest so as to ensure that their combined influence is exercised as effectively as possible through co-ordination, the convergence of their positions and implementation of joint action.

   b) Consultations shall take place before the High Contracting Parties decide on their final position.

   c) In adopting its positions and its national measures each High Contracting Party shall take full account of the positions of the other partners and shall give due consideration to the desirability of adopting and implementing Common European Positions. In order to increase their capacity for joint action in the Foreign Policy Field, the High Contracting Parties shall ensure that common principles and objectives are gradually developed and defined. The determination of Common Positions shall constitute a point of reference for the Policies of the High Contracting parties.

   d) The High Contracting Parties shall endeavour to avoid taking positions which impairs their effectiveness as a cohesive force in international relations or within international organisations.

3. a) The Ministers for Foreign Affairs and a member of the Commission shall meet at least four times a year within the framework of European Political Co-operation. They may also discuss Foreign Policy matters within the framework of political co-operation on the occasion of meetings of the Council of the European Communities.

b) The Commission shall be fully associated with the proceedings of political co-operation.

c) In order to ensure the swift adoption of common positions and the implementation of joint action, the High Contracting Parties shall, as far as possible, refrain from impeding the formation of a consensus and the joint action which this could produce.

4. The High Contracting Parties shall ensure that the European Parliament is closely associated with European Political co-operation. To that end the Presidency shall regularly inform the European Parliament of the Foreign policy issues which are being examined within the framework of political co-operation and shall ensure that the views of the European Parliament are duly taken into consideration.

5. The external policies of the European Community and the policies agreed in European Political Co-operation must be consistent. The Presidency and the Commission, each within its own sphere of competence, shall have special responsibility for ensuring that such consistency is sought and maintained.

6. a) The High Contracting Parties consider that closer co-operation on questions of European Security would contribute in an essential way to the development of a European identity in External Policy matters. They are ready to co-ordinate their positions more closely on the political and economic aspects of security.

b) The High Contracting Parties are determined to maintain the technological and industrial conditions necessary for their security. They shall work to that end both at national level and, where appropriate, within the framework of the competent institutions and bodies.

c) Nothing in this title shall impede closer co-operation in the field of security between certain of the High Contracting Parties within the framework of the Western European Union or the Atlantic Alliance.

7. a) In international institutions and at international conferences which they attend, the High Contracting Parties shall endeavour to adopt common positions on the subjects covered by this title.

b) In international institutions and at international conferences in which not all the High Contracting parties participate, those who do participate shall take full account of positions agreed in European Political Co-operation.

8. The High Contracting Parties shall organise a political dialogue with third countries and regional groupings whenever they deem it necessary.

9. The High Contracting Parties and the Commission, through mutual assistance and information, shall intensify co-operation

between their Representations accredited to third countries and to International Organisations.

10. a) The Presidency of European Political Co-operation shall be held by the High Contracting Party which holds the Presidency of the Council of the European Communities.

   b) The Presidency shall be responsible for initiating action and co-ordinating and representing the positions of the Member States in relations with third countries in respect of European Political Co-operation activities. It shall also be responsible for the management of political co-operation and in particular for drawing up the timetable of meetings and for convening and organising meetings.

   c) The political directors shall meet regularly in the political committee in order to give the necessary impetus, maintain the continuity of European Political Co-operation and prepare Ministers' discussions.

   d) The political committee or, if necessary, a ministerial meeting shall convene within 48 hours at the request of at least three Member States.

   e) The European Correspondents' Group shall be responsible, under the direction of the political committee, for monitoring the implementation of European Political Co-operation and for studying general organisational problems.

   f) Working Groups shall meet as directed by the Political Committee.

   g) A secretariat based in Brussels shall assist the Presidency in preparing and implementing the activities of European Political Co-operation and in administrative matters. It shall carry out its duties under the authority of the Presidency.[5]

The EPC provisions of the Single European Act essentially codified what had developed over the previous two decades. Inevitably the record of the EPC was mixed. On the plus side it led to a habit of cooperation between a whole generation of diplomats traditionally trained to defend the national interest. When desk officers in the Foreign Ministry in London or Paris or Bonn were confronted with a problem it soon became second nature to consult with their colleagues in other capitals, whom they would be meeting in any case every month in Brussels, to find a solution. The SEA created modest but efficient machinery to promote this cooperation and gradually the EC became an increasingly important player on the global scene. On the negative side

5. The full text of the Single European Act may be found in *Treaties Establishing the European Communities*, Office of Official Publications, Luxembourg, 1987.

it was unable to discuss, let alone act together, in the field of military security—the treaty restricted discussion to the political and economic aspects of security. And the need for consensus on every issue often led to the lowest common denominator statement on international issues. There was no agreement on the community versus intergovernmental dispute but a modus operandi had been established to allow the use of Community instruments to support EPC actions.

The experience of the EPC also demonstrated that European foreign policy was not simply the sum of 12 national foreign policies, but rather a unique process with its own features and attributes. When operating with 12 or 15 states, although there are limitations which individual states do not face, at the same time there are considerable benefits to be gained. Another important lesson was the relationship between the internal and external dynamics of the Union. Foreign policy does not stand in splendid isolation. It can only be understood as part of the process of European integration.

Even the improvements made as a result of the SEA could not cope with the dramatic change in European and international affairs following the collapse of communism in Central and Eastern Europe in 1989. The European Commission was tasked with the economic rescue of Central and Eastern Europe by the G7 meeting in Paris in 1989.[6] Yugoslavia was set to implode and the first of several Gulf crises erupted without warning. France and Germany agreed that it was time to move forward and create a common foreign and security policy. The stage was thus set for a new intergovernmental conference (IGC) which would be concluded at Maastricht in 1991. A central element of the IGC would be the establishment of the CFSP.

6.   'G7' stands for 'the Group of Seven' and refers to the meetings at the highest level (Presidents, Prime Ministers, Finance Ministers) of the representatives of the seven major industrial countries: namely Canada, France, Germany, Italy, the United Kingdom and the United States, to discuss economic policy and other issues. Since 1995 Russia has been invited to the political discussions between G7 members and thus the term G8 has come into use. The European Commission is also present at G7/8 meetings.

2 |

The Birth of the CFSP

When the CFSP was negotiated in 1991, it was in answer to a range of
internal and external challenges. France and Germany argued that the
completion of the Single Market and the drive towards economic and
monetary union (EMU) necessitated corresponding moves towards
political union, of which the CFSP was a central element. With the end
of the Cold War, Europe was expected to use its increased weight to
achieve more political influence and ensure stability around its borders.
The limitations of the EPC had been reached and it was necessary to
establish stronger structures for foreign and security policy. There were
thus high expectations for the CFSP that superseded the previous light
framework of the EPC.

The negotiations to establish the CFSP were not easy and reflected
the fundamental differences between those who wished to move
towards a more integrated EU and those who wished to slow down such
moves and ensure that decision-making remained in the hands of the
Member States.[1] The first paper to be published calling for 'a truly
common foreign policy' was that by Belgium in March 1990 in the
lead-up to the Intergovernmental Conference (IGC). It argued for a
stronger and more coherent EU foreign policy and was met with considerable approval in other Member States. The following month
France and Germany addressed a joint message to the Irish Presidency
calling for 'the definition and implementation of a common foreign and
security policy'. The European Council in Dublin decided to add political union to the agenda for the IGC scheduled to start in December
1990 to consider economic and monetary union.

The debates in 1990 identified the main issues that were to be at the
centre of the IGC negotiations on CFSP at both the Maastricht and
Amsterdam IGCs. These included the definition of 'security policy'.

---

1. For a detailed analysis of the CFSP negotiations see Regelsberger (1997).

Did it mean defence? If so, should the Western European Union (WEU) Article V mutual defence guarantee be extended to all Member States? What were the Union's vital common interests? Should foreign and security policy remain under separate institutional procedures?

The Luxembourg Presidency, under pressure from Member States and the European institutions with radically different ideas and perceptions of CFSP, produced a 'non-paper' in April 1991 which was a skilful compromise of the different positions and which effectively was to become the basis of Title V of the new treaty.[2] The Luxembourg draft proposed a European Union based on three pillars: the first for Community matters, the second for the CFSP and the third for justice and home affairs. Decision-making for the CFSP would remain largely intergovernmental but security issues could be discussed and the goal of a common defence policy was mentioned.

When the Dutch took over the Presidency in July 1991 they tried to rewrite the draft treaty in a more community manner but found little support. The final text of the treaty represented a compromise between the advocates of a community approach (eight Member States led by Germany) and those in favour of an intergovernmental approach (four Member States led by the UK and France). Given the need for unanimity at the IGC, the minority in favour of an intergovernmental approach were able to carry the day. A pillar structure was thus established which Commission President Jacques Delors described as a recipe for confusion. Regrettably his forecast was to prove accurate with many disputes in the next years over competencies between the different pillars.

The treaty text also papered over a dispute between the so-called 'Atlanticists' and Europeans with regard to the question of common defence. The British and the Dutch in particular were adamant that there should be nothing in the new treaty which might undermine NATO or put into question the US commitment to Europe's defence.

Title V of the Treaty of Maastricht stated boldly that 'a common foreign and security policy is hereby established covering all areas of foreign and security policy'.[3] The objectives of the CFSP were:

2.   A 'non-paper' is a document circulated by a government or institution without official status. It is usually designed to float new ideas or propose compromise solutions. For an insider account of the Luxembourg handling of the negotiations see Cloos (1994).

3.   The full text of Title V is available on the Europa Server of the European Union (http://www.cc.cec). The text of the CFSP provisions of the Treaty of

- to safeguard the common values, fundamental interests and independence of the Union;
- to strengthen the security of the Union and its Member States in all ways;
- to preserve peace and strengthen international security, in accordance with the principles of the United Nations Charter as well as the principles of the Helsinki Final Act and the objectives of the Paris Charter;
- to promote international cooperation;
- to develop and consolidate democracy and the rule of law, and respect for human rights and fundamental freedoms.

There could be no disagreement about such anodyne 'motherhood and apple pie' aims. The Union was to pursue these objectives by establishing systematic cooperation between Member States and by gradually implementing joint actions in the areas in which the Member States have important interests in common. The Member States were 'to support the Union's external and security policy actively and unreservedly in a spirit of loyalty and mutual solidarity. They shall refrain from any action which is contrary to the interests of the Union or likely to impair its effectiveness as a cohesive force in international relations. The Council shall ensure that these principles are complied with.'

Joint actions and common positions were new features of the CFSP. Joint actions were not defined clearly; they were to be decided by the Council on the basis of general guidelines from the European Council. Whenever the Council decided on the principle of joint action 'it shall lay down the specific scope, the Union's general and specific objectives in carrying out such action, if necessary its duration, and the means, procedures and conditions for its implementation'. There was a cumbersome provision for using augmented qualified majority voting (QMV) in the implementation of joint actions.

Article J.4 was a new departure for the EU. It stated that the CFSP 'shall include all questions related to the security of the Union, including the eventual framing of a common defence policy, which might in time lead to a common defence'. The WEU was described as 'an integral part of the development of the Union' and could be requested 'to elaborate and implement decisions and actions of the Union which have defence implications'. There was to be no QMV for actions having defence implications and acceptance of J.4 'shall not prejudice the

Amsterdam is in Appendix 1. For a comparison of the EPC and CFSP see Cameron (1996).

specific character of the security and defence policy of certain Member States and shall respect the obligations of certain Member States under the North Atlantic Treaty and be compatible with the common security and defence policy established within that framework'.

The Presidency was given an enhanced role. Article J.5 stated that:

(1)   The Presidency shall represent the Union in matters coming within the common foreign and security policy.

(2)   The Presidency shall be responsible for the implementation of common measures; in that capacity it shall in principle express the position of the Union in international organisations and international conferences.

(3)   In the tasks referred to in paragraphs 1 and 2, the Presidency shall be assisted if need be by the previous and next Member States to hold the Presidency. The Commission shall be fully associated in these tasks. [NB the troika]

(4)   With regard to the UN member states which are permanent members of the Security Council will, in the execution of their functions, ensure the defence of the positions and the interests of the Union, without prejudice to their responsibilities under the provisions of the United Nations Charter.

The diplomatic and consular missions of the Member States and the Commission Delegations in third countries and international conferences, and their representations to international organizations, were to cooperate in ensuring that the common positions and common measures adopted by the Council were complied with and implemented. They were also instructed to step up cooperation by exchanging information and carrying out joint assessments.

The position of the European Parliament was given a modest boost. The Presidency was

> to consult the European Parliament on the main aspects and the basic choices of the common foreign and security policy and shall ensure that the views of the European Parliament are duly taken into consideration. The European Parliament shall be kept regularly informed by the Presidency and the Commission of the development of the Union's foreign and security policy. The European Parliament may ask questions of the Council or make recommendations to it. It shall hold an annual debate on progress in implementing the common foreign and security policy.

The Council was 'to ensure the unity, consistency and effectiveness of action by the Union'. The Commission's position was unchanged, being 'fully associated' with the CFSP.

Administrative expenditure for CFSP was to be charged to the budget of the European Communities while operational expenditure could either be charged to the Community budget or from the Member States 'where appropriate in accordance with a scale to be decided'.

Assessment

The changes made under the CFSP chapter were modest, particularly if one compares it to the important steps forward towards EMU. But the EMU decisions had been well prepared by a committee of central bankers under the chairmanship of Commission President Jacques Delors. Nothing similar was ever attempted for foreign and security policy. The CFSP negotiations also took place against the background of the Gulf and Yugoslav crises, and against the doubts of the US about the wisdom of the EU attempting to establish a CFSP with a defence dimension. Not surprisingly there was no attempt to define the CFSP in any detail or to list its priorities.

There were, however, a number of improvements. The European Council became directly involved, not only through the single institutional structure, but also as the body to issue mandates for joint actions. Joint actions and common positions were useful new instruments imposing some discipline and solidarity between Member States. There was an end to the outdated restrictions on discussing the military aspect of security issues; and the introduction of QMV for implementing joint actions, although of more symbolic than of practical value, broke another taboo.

Given the tortured negotiations on Title V and the wide differences between the Member States, it was agreed to review the CFSP at the 1996 IGC. Regrettably the lengthy debate and delay in ratifying the Maastricht Treaty meant that the CFSP could not start before November 1993.

The EU and the Yugoslav Crisis

As the negotiations on the CFSP continued in the second half of 1991, the Yugoslav crisis erupted into war. It is illustrative to look at the EU response to this crisis as Member States were to draw various lessons for reform of the CFSP. These included the difficulties of handling ethnic tensions within fragile states, the dilemmas facing democracies confronted by authoritarian regimes willing to act without restraint, the problems of not backing up diplomacy by credible military force, and the attempts to develop an effective CFSP while preserving Atlantic unity.

The EU is generally regarded as having 'failed' in its attempts to deal with the conflict in former Yugoslavia.[4] This perception was heightened by the exaggerated expectations in 1991 of what the EU could do in 'the hour of Europe'[5] and the constant television images during the following years portraying the horror of war. It is important to remember, however, that until the summer of 1995 there was no political will in the wider international community—the UN, NATO (and particularly the US) to intervene militarily in a decisive manner.

Apart from the IGC negotiations, the EU was confronted with the collapse of communism, which posed strains not only on Yugoslavia but also the Soviet Union and Czechoslovakia. It was also digesting the unification of Germany and facing, together with the US and others, a major challenge to international law in the Gulf with the Iraqi invasion of Kuwait. Ministerial agendas were crowded with meetings dealing with a succession of crises. The precarious situation in the Soviet Union, with Gorbachev under constant threat from hard-liners opposed to *perestroika*, was the issue of most concern to EU ministers. As the Yugoslav crisis developed, ministers were constantly assessing the possible implications of a decision—to recognize Croatia and Slovenia (two constituent republics of Yugoslavia that wished to break away) for example—on the situation in the Soviet Union.

In 1991, the EU was still operating under EPC rules, which specifically excluded any discussion of military security issues. This meant that ministers and officials were not even supposed to discuss the question of the possible use of military force in dealing with the situation in Yugoslavia. Nevertheless, despite EPC restrictions, the question of military intervention was raised in the summer of 1991 and assessments made by both NATO and the WEU as to the numbers required to influence events in Yugoslavia. The assessments from both organizations were that up to 100,000 troops would be required to enforce a ceasefire. Leaving aside the question of political will, the Member States of the EU did not possess these numbers in combat readiness. Only the

4.   Among the best surveys of the fall of Yugoslavia see Silber (1996) and Glenny (1996).

5.   This was the unfortunate phrase used by Luxembourg Foreign Minister Jacques Poos in June 1991.

UK and France had the capability to project power in the region (Germany stated that it was constitutionally unable to act) and London was adamant that it would not become engaged unless the US was involved. But Washington categorically ruled out any US military involvement. The US attitude towards Yugoslavia had a major impact on thinking in European capitals. The Bush administration, experiencing a certain fatigue post-Iraq and post-collapse of communism, was more than content for Europe to deal with the crisis.

As the situation in Yugoslavia worsened, in the spring of 1991 the EU sent Luxembourg's Prime Minister, Jacques Santer, representing the six-monthly rotating EU Presidency, and European Commission President Jacques Delors, to Belgrade to discuss the situation with President Milosevic of Serbia and other regional leaders. The EU leaders were hopeful that Yugoslavia could be preserved and emphasized the importance of resolving disputes by peaceful means, holding out the prospect of increased EU assistance and closer contractual relations. These carrots, however, were insufficient to prevent the march towards conflict and hostilities between Belgrade and Slovenia and Croatia erupted in the final days of June 1991.

The EU's response to the outbreak of fighting included the appointment of Lord Carrington as the EU special representative with a broad mandate to bring the parties to the negotiating table through the Conference on Yugoslavia; the sending of a European Community Monitoring Mission (ECMM) comprising some 200 monitors who did much valuable work and because of their white uniforms became known as the 'ice cream brigade'; efforts to involve the wider international community and in particular the UN; and effecting an arms embargo covering all of Yugoslavia. In the autumn of 1991 there was a consensus within the EU that the constituent republics of Yugoslavia should resolve their future constitutional arrangements themselves by negotiation. The EU had no preconceived ideas as to how these arrangements should look and all efforts were concentrated, therefore, on seeking an end to the fighting and bringing the parties to the negotiating table.

Towards the end of 1991 pressure mounted in Germany to recognize Slovenia and Croatia as independent states. The reasons for this change in the German position included the impact of the huge numbers of refugees (mainly Croatian) who had fled to Germany, pressure from the media and the Catholic Church which had close ties to Croatia and a widespread feeling, post-German unification, that Slovenia and Croatia should be allowed self-determination as had the citizens of East Germany. Partly in response to this pressure, the EU decided to set up a commission under the French constitutional lawyer, Robert Badinter, to assess the criteria for recognition of new states. Chancellor Kohl and Foreign Minister Genscher then increased the stakes by stating—just as the EU Member States were finalizing the Treaty of Maastricht including new provisions to establish a CFSP—that Germany would recognize Slovenia and Croatia before the end of 1991, even in advance of the final Badinter report.[6] This move infuriated Lord Carrington who considered it premature and likely to complicate a comprehensive negotiated solution. But Germany was not isolated for long. The other Member States, including Britain and France, also recognized the two breakaway republics in January 1992.

The decision to recognize Slovenia and Croatia has been sharply criticized but there were pros and cons to consider. On the one hand it led to a halt in the fighting in Croatia, but on the other it opened up the Pandora's box of Bosnia–Herzegovina earlier than might have been expected and gave the EU and others little time to prepare for the conflict there. According to Owen (1995) and Bildt (1998) the EU should have followed the recommendations of Badinter and sought much firmer guarantees for the minority Serbs in Croatia as a precondition of recognition.

In the first half of 1992 the UN began to send troops, the largest contingents being from the UK and France, to support the humanitarian aid efforts in Croatia and later Bosnia. The opening of hostilities in Bosnia further deepened the growing policy rift between the EU and the US. David Owen, who had taken over from Lord Carrington, and Cyrus Vance had reached a deal in late 1992 (the Vance–Owen Plan) that provided for a settlement of the war based on the military realities on the ground. Although it initially supported the deal, the new Clinton administration eventually rejected the plan as unfair to the Muslim

6.   Badinter issued several 'opinions'. In the first he stated that Yugoslavia was 'a state in the process of dissolution'. He later outlined criteria in his various opinions, including respect for minorities, for recognition of new states, under which Croatia would not have qualified but the Former Yugoslavian Republic of Macedonia (FYROM) would have qualified. Most observers consider that it was an error for Badinter to call for a referendum prior to independence for Bosnia-Herzogovina. While it might have had some legal validity, it had fatal political consequences.

Bosnians. The Europeans, with many troops on the ground, were angered at this change in the US position and the different views on both sides of the Atlantic led to the most serious crisis in transatlantic relations since the Alliance was established. Owen (1995: 365) considered the US refusal to endorse the Vance–Owen plan 'a tragedy' which led to an unnecessary prolongation of the war.

Between 1993 and 1995 the conflict in Bosnia was constantly on the agenda of EU foreign ministers and Owen, later to be succeeded by Carl Bildt in June 1995, reported regularly on their efforts to achieve a settlement. Another innovation was the establishment of the Contact Group in April 1994 involving the UK, France, Germany, Russia and the US to discuss the situation in Bosnia and seek to coordinate policy.[7] Despite the involvement of the US and Russia in the Contact Group, the EU was by far the main provider of UN troops and humanitarian aid, and was engaged in the administration of the war-torn city of Mostar.[8]

By 1995 it was clear beyond all doubt that President Milosevic of Serbia would only be prepared to reach an agreement under threat of force. Public opinion on both sides of the Atlantic was sickened by the siege of Sarajevo, the mindless killing of civilians and reports of mass rapes. In August 1995 NATO finally agreed on air strikes against Serbian positions and this, together with a highly successful Croat offensive campaign, led swiftly to the warring parties agreeing to meet at Dayton, Ohio, in the US. The negotiations at Dayton have been well documented by Richard Holbrooke and there is no doubt that it was US engagement and firepower that led to the Dayton Agreement, but it should be noted that the agreement was not significantly different from the earlier Vance–Owen agreement. Although the EU was only marginally involved in Dayton (Neville-Jones 1997) it soon became a key player in the reconstruction efforts. Bildt became the High Representative based in Sarajevo mandated to carry out the decisions of the Peace Implementation Conference.[9]

Could the EU have prevented the Yugoslav war? Leaving aside the flimsy EPC treaty basis under which they were operating, the answer is

7.   Holbrooke (1998) did not attach much importance to the Contact Group.

8.   The administration of Mostar was done under a joint action of the Union. See Chapter 4.

9.   Bildt (1998) has written an account of his time in Sarajevo and drawn some lessons for the EU. Bildt was succeeded by Carlos Westendorp in 1997; Wolfgang Peritisch took over in 1999.

that the Europeans were not capable, alone, in 1991 of acting in a decisive manner. They had been under US leadership and protection for nearly half a century and had not developed any crisis management experience. However, according to Holbrooke (1998: 28), NATO could and should have acted: 'the best chance to prevent war would have been to present the Yugoslavs with a clear warning that NATO airpower would be used against any party that tried to deal with the ethnic tensions of Yugoslavia by force'. Bildt agrees, arguing that while the EU had the ambition but lacked the ability, the reverse applied to NATO. It is impossible to say whether the conflict could have been prevented—certainly not with the limited carrots that Santer and Delors offered in May 1991—but an agreed international policy of limited military measures combined with more radical political initiatives may have produced a peaceful outcome.

One of the main lessons drawn by Owen, Bildt and Holbrooke, and widely shared in the EU, was the need to develop a credible and effective CFSP. It was clear that alone the Member States could achieve little. Bildt (1998: 386) saw national foreign policy as 'often reduced to little more than the occasional photo opportunity and some brave phrases for domestic consumption but with painfully little relevance to affect the realities on the ground'.

The Yugoslav conflict also highlighted the mismatch between the EU's declared foreign policy objectives and the means available to achieve those objectives. In the defence field, despite a total EU GDP similar to the US and defence spending about two-thirds of the US, the European members of NATO were only able to muster about 10% of the long-range deployable military power of the US. As Tony Blair was to argue in late 1998 (see Chapter 6) the absence of an effective European military capability undermined the credibility of the EU in situations such as Bosnia and Kosovo and weakened Europe's position as a partner of the United States.

Another lesson of the Yugoslav crisis was the importance of conflict prevention. As a direct result of the Balkan situation, the French launched an initiative (the Balladur Plan, see Chapter 4) to try to deal with some of the problems between the countries of Central and Eastern Europe (CEEC) in 1993. The lessons of the Yugoslav conflict were never far from the minds of the negotiators at the 1996 IGC preparing improvements in the CFSP.

3 |

CFSP Structures

The CFSP is organized in an inverted pyramid structure. At the apex are the Heads of State and Government meeting at the six monthly European Councils under the rotating Presidency of the Union.[1] The European Council has the responsibility for setting the guidelines for the CFSP and its decisions are important both for substance and for the catalytic effect they have on the policy process. While the European Council has the ultimate authority it rarely has the time to engage in a serious debate on foreign policy. European Council meetings have crowded agendas and can be derailed by lengthy discussion on a current media issue. The campaign to stop the abolition of duty free sales ensured that this subject was discussed for twice as long as Russia at the Portschach European Council in 1998.

Figure 3.1: The CFSP institutions

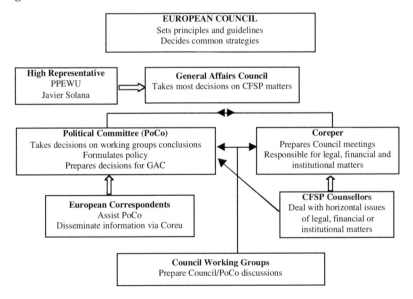

---

1.   See the Glossary for an explanation of CFSP terminology.

The Foreign Affairs Council (also known as the General Affairs Council [GAC]) is the main decision-making body meeting monthly, sometimes more frequently, in Brussels or Luxembourg. It is through this forum that policy options are considered, disagreements addressed and resolved, and foreign policy statements and initiatives issued. The working of the GAC can be affected, however, by the electoral process in Member States, particularly if there are elections in the middle of a half-year Presidency.

The role of the Presidency has evolved significantly. While constrained by the principle of consensus building, individual Presidencies can colour foreign policy priorities. Denmark gave a considerable push to the enlargement process during its 1993 Presidency. During the two 1999 Presidencies, Germany chose Russia as the first EU Common Strategy while Finland promoted the EU's Northern Dimension. A less glamorous but essential role of the Presidency is the efficient organization of business, not only preparing agendas and chairing meetings but also handling an increasing number of political dialogue meetings with third countries and representing the Union in the international forum.

Table 3.1: The rotating presidency

1998	UK, Austria
1999	Germany, Finland
2000	Portugal, France
2001	Sweden, Belgium
2002	Spain, Denmark
2003	Greece

In recent years the number of political dialogue partners of the Union has multiplied. In 1998 there were 156 meetings of the Presidency, troika or the 15 Member States with other third countries or groups of states. By far the most important of these relationships is that with the US which comprises not only six monthly summit meetings but also regular ministerial and senior official consultations as well as a proliferation of contacts at working group level.[2] Similar but less intense dialogues are held with Canada, Japan, China, Australia, India, Pakistan, South Korea and many other countries. There are also provisions for political dialogue with all of the Union's neighbours including the

2.   See Gardner (1997) for the development of EU–US relations under the New Transatlantic Agenda.

European Economic Area (EEA) countries, the Mediterranean countries through the Barcelona process, the CEECs, Russia, Ukraine and other newly independent states. An increasing tendency has been 'group to group' dialogues with the EU engaging with regional groupings such as the Association of South-East Asian Nations (ASEAN), the Gulf Cooperation Council, and, from Latin America, the Rio Group and Mercosur.[3]

Table 3.2: Council CFSP Working Groups

Title	Acronym
Latin America	COLAT
Asia/Oceania	COASI
Ad hoc – Middle East Peace Process	COMEP
Mashrek/Maghreb	COMAG
Middle East/Gulf	COMEM
OSCE	COSCE
Central Europe	COCEN
Eastern Europe and Central Asia	COEST
Ad hoc – Former Yugoslavia	COYUG
South East Europe (Turkey, Cyprus, Malta, Albania)	COSEE
Africa	COAFR
Consular affairs	COCON
Drugs	CODRU
Terrorism	COTER
CFSP Administrative affairs	COADM
Protocol	COPRO
Disarmament	CODIS
United Nations	CONUN
Security	COSEC
Public International Law	COJUR
Analysis and Forecasting	COPLA
Non-proliferation	CONOP
Exports of conventional arms	COARM
CFSP Communications	COTEL
Human rights	COHOM

3.   ASEAN membership includes Brunei, Cambodia, China, Indonesia, Laos, Malaysia, Myanmar, Philippines, Singapore, Taiwan, Thailand and Vietnam. The GCC includes Bahrain, Kuwait, Oman, Qatar, Saudi Arabia and the United Arab Emirates. The Rio Group includes Argentina, Bolivia, Brazil, Chile, Colombia, Ecuador, Mexico, Paraguay, Peru and Uruguay. Mercosur includes Argentina, Paraguay, Uruguay and Brazil.

The Political Committee also meets monthly and takes decisions that do not require ministerial approval. The Presidency chairs meetings and sets the agenda for CFSP meetings while the minutes are taken by the Council Secretariat. The European Correspondents are the real hub of the CFSP machinery, being the link persons in foreign ministries who ensure that telegrams are circulated, replies sent out and ministers briefed on CFSP issues. Most Member States have a CFSP department that supports the European Correspondent. A large number of Working Groups (in 1999 over 25) covering regional and functional issues then meet at regular intervals, also in Brussels, to prepare reports for the Political Committee.

Table 3.3 covers the agenda of the first meeting of the working group on the Western Balkans (COWEB) during the Finnish Presidency.

Table 3.3: COWEB-Meeting of the Western Balkans Region Working Group, Brussels, 1 July 1999

Workplan for the Finnish Presidency

Kosovo
 • Civil implementation and reconstruction; EU's role
Policies towards FRY/Kosovo
Stability Pact
 • Meeting of Heads of State and Government
 • First meeting of the Regional Table
 • Joint action
CFSP Special Envoys
 • Future needs in FRY and Kosovo
Albania
 • Preparation of Friends of Albania, 22 July
FYROM
 • Report by Ambassador Ahrens, policy recommendations
Bosnia and Herzegovina
 • Political dialogue
 • Interpretation of the provisions of the Common Position 96/184/CFSP
Croatia
 • Political dialogue
ECMM
 • Presentation by the new ECMM Head of Mission
 • Budget for the Finnish Presidency
Common Strategy for Western Balkans (information).

In addition to these meetings, normally held in Brussels, there is a constant flow of information circulated by the CFSP telegraphic network known as Coreu traffic. There has been a steady increase in the number of Coreus sent, from 15,432 in 1992 to 20,721 in 1995 and 24,680 in 1998. This flood of paper covers both administrative arrangements such as who will participate in meetings, exchange of information on visits to and from third countries as well as policy papers on which partners are invited to comment.

Given the unanimity rule in CFSP, it inevitably becomes increasingly difficult to arrive at a consensus. With 15 Member States, plus the Commission, policy discussions can be lengthy affairs. These are problems that will become worse as a result of further enlargement, unless changes are made to the system.

There is a small but growing acquis—body of rules, precedents and legislation—in the CFSP area covering the principles of CFSP, the joint actions in place (for example, sanctions on a number of countries), the arrangements for political dialogue with third countries, and so on. The new Member States will have to accept this acquis in full but the results of the initial talks with the candidate countries in 1998 revealed few problems in this area.

The Council

As a result of the Maastricht Treaty, the formerly autonomous EPC Secretariat was integrated into the Council Secretariat and a CFSP unit established within the External Relations Directorate General (DGE). In 1999 it had around 70 staff, half being European civil servants and half being national officials on secondment, organized also on geographic and thematic lines. Their main function was to provide support services for the Presidency by preparing and sending out notices of meetings, taking notes and providing a central memory for CFSP. This is particularly important in managing the multiplicity of political dialogue meetings with third countries.

Under the Maastricht Treaty, the Council Secretariat had no mandate to play a policy role in the CFSP but this was changed as a result of the Treaty of Amsterdam. The Secretary General (Mr CFSP) has been tasked 'to assist the Council in matters coming within the scope of CFSP, in particular through contributing to the formulation, preparation and implementation of policy decisions, and, when appropriate, and acting on behalf of the Council at the request of the Presidency, through conducting political dialogue with third parties' (Article J.16). He will also head the new policy planning and early warning unit (PPEWU, see Appendix 4).[4]

Figure 3.2: Structure of the Council: External Affairs

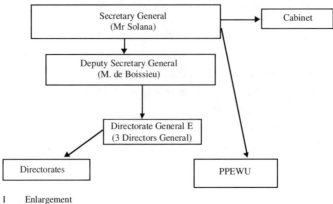

I   Enlargement
II   Development
III   Multilateral Economic Affairs
IV   Transatlantic Relations, UN, Human Rights
V   SE Europe, Mediterranean, Middle East
VI   Asia, Latin America, Africa
VII   W. Balkans, NIS, Central and Eastern Europe
VIII   Security
IX   General Affairs

Note: Mr CFSP works under the authority of the Presidency. The exact location of the PPEWU was to be decided when Mr Solana took up his responsibilities towards the end of 1999.

The Council has two small overseas offices, in New York and Geneva, which liaise with the Presidency *sur place* and the United Nations. The possibility of extending the Council's overseas offices has been mooted but this would complicate even further the external representation of the Union.

4.   Javier Solana was appointed as the first Mr CFSP in June 1999. He had previously been Foreign Minister of Spain and Secretary General of NATO. He was replaced as Secretary General of NATO by George Robertson, the British Defence Minister. The traditional functions of the Secretary General of the Council are to be taken over by the Deputy Secretary General.

The Commission

The Commission's role during the EPC years was ambiguous. The Member States were reluctant to grant the Commission speaking rights while the Commission was keen to protect its 'Community turf'. The Commission's role was recognized in the 1987 SEA as being 'fully associated' with the EPC and this formula was maintained under the CFSP. Member States recognized that they could not implement EPC or CFSP actions without recourse to Community instruments such as sanctions, and hence the important role of the Commission was recognized in the Maastricht treaty.

Following the establishment of the CFSP, the Commission moved to reorganize its external services. During the final two years of the Delors Commission Presidency, 1993–94, Sir Leon Brittan was responsible for external economic affairs and Hans van den Broek for external political affairs, including CFSP. It soon became clear that this division of responsibilities was less than satisfactory and with the appointment of Jacques Santer as President of the Commission, the decision was taken to further reorganize the external services. The new structure (1995–99) was as follows:

- DG1 (Sir Leon Brittan) responsible for commercial policy, relations with North America, the Far East, Australia and New Zealand.
- DG1A (Hans van den Broek) responsible for Europe and the NIS (former Soviet Union), the CFSP and external missions
- DG1B (Manuel Marin) responsible for the Southern Mediterranean, Middle East, Latin America, South-East Asia, and North–South Cooperation
- DGVIII (João de Deus Pinheiro) responsible for development co-operation with Africa, the Caribbean and the Pacific, plus the Lomé Convention.

In addition to these four Commissioners, two others had direct involvement in external affairs. Emma Bonino was given responsibility inter alia for the European Community Humanitarian Office (ECHO), and Yves Thibault de Silguy's economic affairs portfolio included some competencies for international economic policy.

In a novel approach to handling the Commission, President Santer invited these six Commissioners to meet regularly under his chairmanship to discuss and coordinate external policy. This group became known as the Relex Group of Commissioners. The regular meetings of the Relex groups served a useful coordination function and was supposed to, but rarely did, provide a forum to hold in-depth discussions of issues only of relevance to those dealing with external affairs such as the external service of the Commission, sanctions policy, geo-political implications of enlargement and the external relations aspects of the IGC.

DG1A was the Directorate General created specifically to deal with the CFSP. Established out of the small EPC directorate which had been part of the Secretariat General of the Commission, the new DG expanded rapidly. At the end of 1998 DG1A was responsible for a network of 127 delegations around the world, employing 729 staff in Brussels and 2452 overseas (622 Brussels-based and 1830 locally-based staff)— on some estimates the fifth largest diplomatic service in Europe. The tasks of these delegations are tailored to local circumstances but they all provide valuable reporting which enhances the Commission's standing in external affairs.

During 1999, partly as a result of the entry into force of the Amsterdam Treaty and partly as a result of the Commission's resignation, there was a further reorganization of the Commission's external services. The new Commission President, Romano Prodi, decided to divide external affairs into five areas of responsibility as shown in Figure 3.3. This division meant that Prodi had decided against the establishment of a Vice President for External Affairs which was foreseen in a protocol to the Amsterdam Treaty.

Figure 3.3: Structure of the Commission in External Affairs

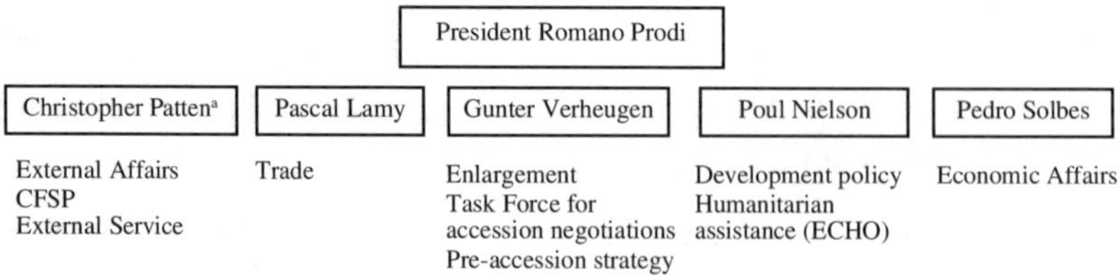

President Romano Prodi				
Christopher Patten[a]	Pascal Lamy	Gunter Verheugen	Poul Nielson	Pedro Solbes
External Affairs CFSP External Service	Trade	Enlargement Task Force for accession negotiations Pre-accession strategy	Development policy Humanitarian assistance (ECHO)	Economic Affairs

[a] Mr Patten was to chair a group of the above Commissioners dealing with external affairs. The group was to coordinate the external policies of the Commission, ensure coherence of overall policy and define strategic priorities.

The European Parliament (EP)

The European Parliament's rights in CFSP are akin to those of national parliaments and are limited to consultation and information by the Presidency and Commission. It also has the important power to ratify new treaties and agreements concluded with third countries. Although it has limited staff and expertise in foreign affairs, the EP has devoted more and more attention to foreign policy in recent years. There are increasing 'hearings' with outside experts and both the Presidency and the Commission have been assiduous in the provision of regular briefings to the full EP and its committees dealing with external affairs. Unlike in other areas, where it received increased powers, the role of the EP in the CFSP was not changed as a result of IGC decisions at Amsterdam, but in due course it may gain a greater influence through the new 'Community' arrangements for financing the CFSP.[5] In July 1999 the German Christian Democrat MEP, Elmar Brok, was appointed chairman of the Foreign Affairs Committee.

Figure 3.4: The European Parliament and the CFSP

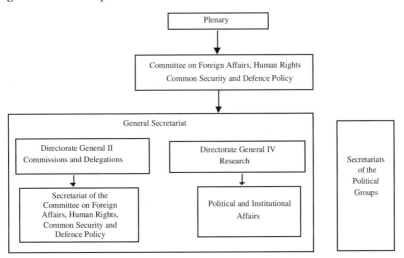

5. Gourlay (1999) analyses ways in which the EP may strengthen its influence in the CFSP area. The annual reports of the EP on CFSP have steadily improved over the years. See, for example, the Spencer report of 2 March 1999 (POLI/DT/ 370/370576).

The External Budget

It is difficult to operate a foreign policy without money. Just under 6% of the Union's 86.5 billion Euro budget for 1999 was earmarked for external affairs. The bulk of spending—some 2 billion Ecus—was earmarked for Central and Eastern Europe, Russia and the NIS, with a further 900 Mecu for North Africa and the Mediterranean. Food aid totalled some 850 Mecu, with another 730 Mecu for development aid, followed by 550 Mecu for specific development projects in Cuba, Vietnam, Latin America and Africa. Much of these sums were to be disbursed by the European Community Humanitarian Aid Office (ECHO). Other priorities in recent years have included supporting the transition in South Africa (125 Mecu), monitoring the elections in Palestine (80 Mecu), administering the Bosnian town of Mostar (32 Mecu). In what is perhaps a sign of how immature the CFSP remains, its administrative budget line in 1999 was a mere 30 Mecu. But the Kosovo conflict and the reconstruction efforts in the Balkans were certain to lead to an increased budgetary appropriation for external affairs. The growing number of EU special envoys is also likely to lead to increased provisions to enable them to fulfil their mandates.

4 |

The CFSP in Operation

Since the Treaty on European Union (TEU) came into operation on 1 November 1993, the EU has agreed a number of joint actions including monitoring elections and supporting democracy in Russia, South Africa,[1] Palestine, Nigeria and the Congo; the provision of humanitarian assistance in former Yugoslavia and establishing an administration for Mostar; supporting the Middle East Peace Process including the sending of a special envoy; lobbying jointly for the extension of the Non-Proliferation Treaty (NPT); agreeing export guidelines for the use of dual use goods; agreement on policy towards export and control of anti-personnel mines; promoting the Stability Pact to tackle problems concerned with borders/minorities in Central and Eastern Europe; supporting the civilian nuclear plant (KEDO) in North Korea; and legislation to counter US claims on extra-territoriality.

In addition to these joint actions, a number of common positions (i.e. alignment of policies but not necessarily taking action together or committing resources) have been adopted on former Yugoslavia (e.g. bans on arms exports, flights, investments), Libya, Sudan, Haiti, Rwanda, Ukraine, Burundi, Angola, East Timor, Afghanistan, Iraq, Nigeria, Cuba, Albania, Sierre Leone and Belarus. In addition there have been common positions on the grouping of diplomatic missions, on biological and chemical weapons, on the prevention of conflicts; and decisions regarding the functioning and financing of the CFSP, communications in the CFSP, political dialogue commitments and a code of conduct on arms exports. All these joint actions, common positions and decisions, including the decisions of successive European Councils on CFSP, add up to a substantial and serious acquis on CFSP.

While these actions have been useful in coordinating the positions of Member States on some key issues, they have not led to increased EU

---

1.   The joint action towards South Africa has been well documented in Holland (1995b).

visibility nor really decisive action. The scope has been modest and the added value of the CFSP not always apparent. The most visible failures have been in Yugoslavia and, to a lesser extent, in Rwanda.

It is perhaps worth examining three of the first joint actions, the Stability Pact, the administration of Mostar and the Non-Proliferation Treaty, in more detail, to see how the CFSP operates in practice.

The Stability Pact

It was the difficulties faced by the Union in Yugoslavia that prompted France to launch the idea for a Stability Pact in the spring of 1993. French officials, concerned about the EU's failure to anticipate the crisis and alarmed at the outbreak of ethnic violence in former Yugoslavia, put forward proposals for the Union to use its influence on the Central and East European candidates for membership of the EU to help them resolve their border and minority disputes. The proposal was officially launched by the French Prime Minister, Edouard Balladur, in June 1993.[2] The Copenhagen European Council that same month welcomed the 'Balladur Plan' and agreed that it should be one of the first joint actions of the CFSP.

The Brussels European Council of October 1993 set out the main elements of the initiative, defining the Pact as:

> – an exercise of preventive diplomacy with the EU playing an active and catalytic role. Its aim was to promote good neighbourly relations and to encourage countries to consolidate frontiers and resolve problems of national minorities;
> – a project with a geographically open and evolutionary nature. It would initially focus on the countries of Central and Eastern Europe (CEEC) with the perspective of accession;
> – any agreements reached in the course of the negotiations and the accompanying measures offered by the Union would constitute the main elements of the Pact;
> – an initiative based on existing UN, OSCE and Council of Europe principles. No new institution would be created and the Pact would be transferred to the OSCE.[3]

The Launching Conference in Paris, 26–27 May 1994, stated that the aim was 'to encourage countries which have not yet concluded co-

2.   For the best exposé of French motives, see the interview with Mr Balladur in *Le Monde*, 11 June 1993.

3.   Conclusions of the European Council, October 1993.

operation and good neighbourliness agreements...to do so through a process of bilateral negotiation and regional tables, the composition and agenda for which will have been freely chosen by the participating countries'. The objectives of the roundtables were to be:

> the identification of arrangements and projects aimed at facilitating the achievement and the realisation of agreements and measures for good neighbourly relations in areas such as regional trans-border co-operation, questions relating to minorities, cultural co-operation including language training, economic co-operation, legal co-operation and administrative training, environmental problems.[4]

At the outset expectations for the success of the initiative were not very high. Nearly all of the (nine) countries towards which the Pact was directed harboured reservations, and in some cases resentment, at having been chosen as 'principally concerned countries' in an initiative built upon the premise that disputes in their region over frontiers and minorities posed a threat to European peace and stability. Among the criticisms voiced was concern that the Balladur Plan was mainly an instrument of French domestic politics, designed to raise the Prime Minister's profile in external relations. This criticism was given added justification by the French determination to hold the concluding conference in Paris during their Presidency and just a month before the presidential elections. This created concern that France's intentions might lead to undermining the Organization for Security and Cooperation in Europe (OSCE); concern that the French initiative was designed to keep the US out of European security issues; about duplication of efforts (some bilateral treaties between Central and Eastern European countries had already been agreed); about the paternalistic attitude of the EU (why only touch on problems in Central and Eastern Europe—and not Western Europe?); and about dragging sensitive bilateral issues into a multilateral forum, in which there were many (unaffected) participants.

The Union also had to work hard to dispel the perception in some quarters that the Pact was intended as an obstacle to keep the CEECs out of the Union. An initial French text had stated 'that no enlargement of the EU could occur unless the applicants had settled their problems (borders and minorities) which could threaten stability in Europe'. For some, this was interpreted as an additional condition to those laid down

---

4. Conclusions of the GAC, 12 December 1994.

at the Copenhagen European Council in June 1993, particularly the clause stating that accession required candidates to demonstrate that they had stable institutions guaranteeing democracy, the rule of law, respect for and protection of minorities. In the ad hoc High Level Group established to monitor the progress of the Pact, the language was changed, at the suggestion of the Commission, as follows: 'the perspective of accession is an essential incentive in encouraging the CEECs to settle their differences in bilateral agreements and to abide by them. This should be presented as a logical outcome to the Copenhagen European Council, not as a new condition'. This presentational aspect was highly important in diminishing the fears of some CEECs about EU motives concerning linkage between the Pact and eventual accession to the EU.

There was further suspicion in the OSCE and, to a lesser extent, in the Council of Europe that the Union was trying to establish a rival organization that would undermine their work. The Union went out of its way to reassure both organizations that the Pact was designed to strengthen and not weaken their efforts. A number of meetings were held at an early stage with senior officials of the OSCE, including the High Commissioner for National Minorities, and Council of Europe to explain the reason for the initiative.

There were also doubts, particularly in Moscow and Washington, about the Union's capacity to organize and run such an extensive diplomatic operation. Russia was initially rather lukewarm towards the Pact, preferring to use existing OSCE mechanisms rather than play along to the EU's fiddle. It required some sensitive negotiation to persuade Russia to participate in the Baltic roundtable but it eventually participated in a positive manner. The US was equally lukewarm in the beginning and rather strangely made its participation in the Pact dependent on Russia's involvement.

There was also some debate whether to extend the geographical scope of the Pact, for example, to war-torn Yugoslavia, but it was recognized that this would run counter to other efforts, notably the EU/UN-sponsored Peace Conference, and risked derailing the entire operation. Furthermore, the idea of the Pact was 'preventative diplomacy' not crisis management or resolution. In the course of the roundtable negotiations, these doubts and fears were gradually allayed. The Union was able to persuade the nine principally concerned countries and their neighbours to sit down together and constructively discuss the problems of the region, including subjects which for some were taboo, such as borders and minorities.

The two roundtables covering the Baltics and the CEECs, were the centre-stage of EU diplomatic activity concerning the Pact. Prior to, and indeed between sessions of the roundtables, there were numerous bilateral visits and meetings designed to remove problems and consider solutions. The EU operated initially under the Presidency/Commission tandem and then the troika[5] formula was used as the principal diplomatic instrument that involved travelling frequently around the region for bilateral and multilateral contacts.

Following a meeting between the EU and the nine principally concerned countries in Athens in February 1994, a number of guidelines were established. First, the EU would play an active role as moderator of the roundtables. Secondly, participation in each roundtable would depend on regional circumstances and the capacity of other countries or international institutions to contribute to the outcome. Thirdly, there would be no discussion of changing borders, rather Helsinki principles concerning the inviolability of borders would be reiterated.[6] However, there would be measures taken to promote good neighbourliness including facilitating cross-border communication.

Not all countries were involved to the same extent. The two principal areas of concern were the Baltics, involving mainly Estonia and Latvia (Lithuania has less than 10% Slavic minority compared to between 40 and 50% for its two neighbouring states), and south-east Europe, involving mainly Hungary, Slovakia and Romania. Poland, the Czech Republic and Bulgaria sometimes found it difficult to disguise their lack of interest. In early 1994 there was a suggestion from the US that Ukraine might be included as a principally concerned country in the roundtables. This was rejected on the grounds that Ukraine was not a candidate for EU membership but Ukraine did participate in the roundtable at the invitation of the principally concerned countries.

5.   The troika is a misnomer in that there are always four participants—the current Presidency of the Council, the immediate past and the immediate following Presidency, plus the ever present Commission. The troika formula may be used at ministerial or official level. Note that the composition of the troika was changed as a result of the Amsterdam Treaty.

6.   There had been reference in Balladur's *Le Monde* interview to the possibility of minor border changes. It was quickly recognized that proceeding down this track could create problems, and hence the idea was dropped.

A key issue in the Baltic roundtable was whether or not Russia would participate either as a full or observer member. Sustained efforts eventually persuaded Russia to engage, initially as an observer, and later as a full member in the work of the Baltic roundtable. As a result, the roundtable contributed significantly to a thawing of relations between the Baltic States and Russia, with these countries entering into a useful dialogue on a number of contentious issues such as rights of the large Russian minorities in Latvia and Estonia, and Russian transit from Kaliningrad through Lithuania. The first meeting on 21 September 1994 in Brussels was marked by a constructive atmosphere, aided by the completion of the withdrawal of Russian troops from the Baltic states. The meeting came up with a number of new proposals for accompanying measures and Russia confirmed that it would upgrade its participation at the following meeting on 1 December in Copenhagen. The US welcomed this move as its participation was tied to Russian involvement. The roundtable did not make progress on all fronts. Estonian relations with Russia remained strained because of the continuing border dispute and the new Estonian citizenship law, while Latvian–Russian relations were also strained because of disagreement over the inspection regime at Skrunda military base and military pensioners. Nevertheless a number of other important bilateral treaties and agreements were concluded during the lifetime of the Pact, notably those between Poland and Lithuania, Belarus and Lithuania, and Latvia and Russia.

In contrast to the first meeting of the Baltic roundtable, the opening meeting of the Central and Eastern European roundtable was rather difficult with a number of countries expressing concern that the EU was not prepared to make additional resources available for Stability Pact projects. 'The Nine' were invited to put forward proposals for accompanying measures and among their suggestions were minority language training, assistance to improve border crossings and training of border/customs personnel. A number of CEECs were also opposed to discussing the inclusion of bilateral treaties in the roundtables.

Gradually the mistrust was dispelled and the roundtable meetings plus the troika's travels played a large part in the improvement of Hungary's troubled relations with neighbouring Romania and Slovakia, culminating, in the latter case, in the signature of a historic bilateral treaty of good neighbourly relations on the eve of the Final Conference. The Concluding Conference was held in Paris on 20–21 March 1995 with a full turnout of foreign ministers from OSCE states. The conference endorsed a concluding document that drew attention to the Stability Pact's achievements and listed all the accompanying measures which had been drawn up by the Commission.

The Stability Pact can fairly be described as a success for the CFSP of the Union. The EU was the author, pilot and engine of an ambitious pan-European initiative aimed at strengthening security and stability in Central and Eastern Europe. Apart from convening three high-profile conferences bringing together the foreign ministers of all OSCE countries, the Union chaired seven rounds of each regional roundtable and guided the negotiation of two political declarations adopted by over 50 states.

By careful diplomacy the Union succeeded in persuading the organizations on whose principles the initiative was founded, the OSCE and the Council of Europe, that its intention was not to undermine them but rather to promote the implementation of their standards and to give fresh impetus to their work. The Union went out of its way to avoid giving the impression of dictating to the OSCE, the organization destined to be the guardian of the Pact. The Pact was therefore a vehicle for furthering the objective of increasing the extent to which the various European institutions reinforce one another.

The European Commission made an important contribution to the success of the Pact by a judicious use of carrots, under the PHARE technical assistance programmes for the region. The Commission prepared a list of 'Accompanying Measures' containing about $300 million of projects ranging from measures to improve regional cooperation such as improvements to border crossings, to the promotion of minority languages.

As regards the Central and East Europeans, their initial cool response was transformed within a year to one of general welcome and support for the Pact. They became less suspicious, more relaxed and open about discussing previous taboo subjects in front of a multilateral audience. This was an important achievement.

It is possible to identify a number of factors which contributed to the overall success of the Pact. First, the common political will of the Union to see the initiative through to a successful conclusion. This meant that, despite changes in the Council Presidency, the momentum and direction of the diplomatic process was maintained throughout the period of the Pact's life. The fact that the Joint Action sought to facilitate the achievement of a clear strategic objective agreed by the European Council, that is the progressive integration of the CEECs into the Union, sustained the sense of common purpose that kept the project on-track during the difficult periods. Bilateral diplomatic lobbying by many Member States and the Commission complemented the formal work of the troika on behalf of the Union.[7]

Secondly, the joint action was directed towards those countries where the Union had considerable political and economic leverage, thereby maximizing the prospects of achieving its objectives. Although the Union did not make the Pact a precondition of enlargement to the east, it was clear to the associated countries that the process of integration into the Union was linked to their progress in resolving any outstanding problems with their neighbours. This ensured their continued cooperation. As an incentive, PHARE-funded accompanying measures were of secondary importance to the perspective of membership, particularly as the Union decided not to provide additional resources.

Finally, the Union chose to work in cooperation with other European bodies, rather than in competition with them. This allowed results to be achieved which would not have been possible if the EU had decided to go it alone.

The model of the Stability Pact was used in 1999 as the basis for the Stability Pact for south-east Europe. As with the CEECs, the perspective of closer relations with the EU was seen as an important incentive for the countries of the western Balkans to cooperate with each other. In addition the south-east Europe model also embraced elements of the Helsinki OSCE baskets—democracy, economic reform and security issues.

The EU Administration of Mostar (EUAM)

Following the establishment of the Muslim–Croat Bosnian Federation in March 1994 the EU Member States believed that involvement in one of the cities most affected by the fighting between the Bosnian Croats and Muslims (additionally the second largest city of the Federation) would help rebuild Croat-Bosnian cooperation and thereby strengthen the Federation. Consequently, the Council of Ministers formally deci-

---

7.   It should be noted that in November 1994 the Council of Europe produced a draft convention on minorities which was passed to the various participants in the Pact.

ded on 16 May 1994 on a joint action with the aim of supporting the administration of the City of Mostar.[8] The Council Decision provided for an initial assessment mission and budget of up to 32 million ECU.

Before the war, Mostar was known for its ethnic diversity. With a population of 127,000 Muslims and Croats were nearly equal in population, and a sizeable Serbian minority comprised 19% of the inhabitants. In May 1993, after Croats and Bosnians jointly challenged the Serbian siege of Mostar, Croats turned against Muslims and began a bloody ten-month 'war within the war'. Both peoples defended Mostar as the place of their cultural heritage and used torture, forced expulsion, violation and murder to defend it. The Croats pursued the aim of controlling Mostar as the capital of their independent Republic of Herceg-Bosna. The result was the expulsion of 13,000 Muslims and the destruction of East Mostar.

When the EUAM began its work on 23 July 1994, the population had shrunk to about 60,000 and was strictly divided into the 70% destroyed East, controlled by the Muslims, and the less damaged, Croat-controlled West. After three weeks of difficult negotiations with both military commanders of the town, demilitarization was carried out under the auspices of the Spanish United Nations Protection Force (UNPROFOR) troops just before the establishment of the EUAM.

The EUAM team started working in very difficult conditions, such as sporadic shelling of the city by Serbs from the mountains only 3 km away from town, the ruined state of most of East Mostar, the suffering of the population during and after the phases of open conflict, the breakdown of normal services and the collapse of the economy.

The EUAM drew its mandate from the Memorandum of Understanding (MoU) signed on 5 July 1994, by the EU, WEU and the various parties involved in the former conflict.[9]

8.   Council decision of 16 May 1994 (94/308/CFSP). This decision followed an earlier joint action on 8 November 1993 (Council Decision 93/603/CFSP) to support the convoying of humanitarian aid to Bosnia and Herzegovina but the situation on the ground in winter 1993/94 with the Bosnian Serb forces hindering access for the humanitarian aid convoys meant that the initially proposed joint action could not be implemented.

9.   The representatives of the former conflicting parties were at the local level the Mayors of West and East Mostar, Mijo Brajkovic and Safet Orucevic, the President of the Republic of Bosnia and Herzegovina, Alija Izetbegovic at the national level, Haris Silajdzic for the Federation and Jadranko Prlic as the representative of the Bosnian Croats.

The MoU set out various aims and principles to be achieved by the EUAM including:

- to give the parties time to find a lasting solution for the administration of Mostar;
- to contribute to a climate leading to a single, self-sustaining and multi-ethnic administration of the city;
- to hold democratic elections before the end of EUAM;
- to assist in the return to normal life in the city;
- to restore public utilities;
- to ensure the protection of human rights;
- to enable the return of refugees and displaced persons;
- to assist in organizing and providing humanitarian aid;
- to prepare and implement programs for economic reconstruction;
- to ensure the maintenance of public order;
- to re-establish all public functions and to ensure the national, religious and cultural identity of all the people in the area under EU Administration in compliance with the Constitution of the Federation of Bosnia and Herzegovina.

Although the objectives in the MoU were not quantified, they were wide-ranging and ambitious within the situation of continuing conflict, ongoing mistrust and tension between the parties. The aims and principles were further developed in a strategy document of 13 May 1995 and prepared by Hans Koschnik, the Administrator. Although the EUAM was not explicitly required to achieve a single administration for Mostar, the EU position was clear that a single administration remained its fundamental goal. The main criteria in the EUAM strategy document considered essential to the concept of a unified city included:

- a population willing to live under a common set of rules;
- a central municipal authority acceptable to the population;
- a common legal framework and guaranteed rights for all citizens independent of religion, language and culture;
- a common public service, tax system and police force;
- freedom of movement.

The principal assumptions against which the overall EUAM strategy document was prepared was that:

- the Federation between the Bosnians and the Bosnian-Herzegovinan Croats would remain intact and further developed;

- the United Nations Protection Force (UNPROFOR) would remain in the region with its existing strength unchanged;
- the shelling of Mostar by the Bosnian Serb Army (BSA) would not reach a level that rendered the task of the EU Administration impossible;
- the EUAM would progressively gain the confidence of the citizens of Mostar and not be obstructed in achieving its aims and objectives by any of the different parties.

The MoU stated that Mostar would be governed by the EUAM for a maximum of two years and that the Administrator would be the head of the city municipality. He would have the powers necessary to fulfil the aims and principles of the EUAM while administering the Mostar city municipality properly and efficiently and in correspondence with the views and wishes of the local parties and population. In exchange, the receiving parties would assure the unrestricted commitment to support the EU-Administrator in the exercise of his duties. The Administrator would receive his instructions from the Council of Ministers and would operate in consultation and close collaboration with the local parties.

One of the top priorities for the EUAM was the provision of housing. In the first two years EUAM provided for the reconstruction of 5600 dwellings, 420 houses and 16 apartment blocks for about 30,000 beneficiaries, which was an essential contribution to the city's recovery. In other areas there were mixed results. There was some success in restoring public utilities but joint projects like the local bus company and the repair of the hydro-electric power plants were less successful owing to reservations on both sides. Freedom of movement was hindered by both sides, thus inhibiting economic recovery. Although the restoration and reorganization of health and social services to meet the basic needs of medical and social care in the city was a success, the EUAM's intention of promoting the reunification of the two health services, with the Bijeli Brijeg central hospital as the most crucial project, was not achieved. Neither was there a return to mixed schools in the educational sector. In the early phase of the EUAM, humanitarian aid provided the citizens of Mostar on both sides with such basic needs as food and heating supplies.

According to the MoU, a Unified Police Force of Mostar (UPFM) was to be established with the support of 182 WEU police officers to ensure public safety and freedom of movement in a unified city. Coordination of the UPFM was the first task the EU had delegated to the

WEU since ratification of the Maastricht Treaty (TEU), which called on the WEU to 'elaborate and implement decisions and actions of the Union which have defense implications'. The WEU was 'to seek to restore and maintain peace, confidence, and individual civil rights within the overall mandate of the EUAM'. Furthermore, the WEU was to build a framework that would ensure a smooth transition of the UPFM to local control when the WEU and EU mandate expired. The EUAM experienced major difficulties in achieving progress towards the UPFM, despite this having been earlier identified as one of the most important tasks agreed in the MoU, as a result of Croat and Muslim intransigence. Almost all actions of the EUAM were linked to the freedom of movement. However, the Croats' constant obstruction was detrimental to their efforts and only international pressure from the highest political level, in close cooperation with Croatian President Tudjman, finally brought full freedom of movement—at least on paper. The elections were the last major goal of the EUAM before its original mandate expired. Each side tried to jeopardize the outcome of the elections fearing domination by the other ethnic group. The elections were held and provided the essential basis for a return to local rule.

The Mostar joint action was both extremely ambitious and difficult because of the lack of cooperation between the parties and the lack of EU experience in running such an operation. The Council rushed into the Mostar Administration without any preliminary doctrine or systematic plan on how to deal with postwar reconstruction or peace-building activities. The six-month rotation in the Council Presidency was not best suited to the need for continuity in management of a joint action such as Mostar. The personnel responsible for the ultimate decisions and their execution changed every six months, and, as is normal with the functioning of the Presidency of the Council, not only does the apparatus shift from one Member States capital to another as the Presidency rotates, but each Presidency sets different priorities. This leads to a lack of coherence in dealing with particular issues. In addition, the assisting Working Party had numerous other responsibilities and often decisions were carried over from one meeting to the next, reflecting the need to refer back to Member State capitals. Despite these problems considerable progress was achieved in the areas of rehabilitation, reconstruction and redevelopment. Most projects proceeded smoothly, but a number were delayed for various political and technical reasons, leading to a time lapse between project initiation and execution.

Notwithstanding these problems, the reconstruction of the city was ultimately an enormous success. The more difficult objective was to unite the city politically and socially in order to prepare its residents for self-administration. The Croats constantly rejected any progress towards political reunification of the city, even though they had committed themselves under the MoU to support the EU Administration. Overall the joint action may be judged a success, not least against the very likely horrendous consequences of what would have occurred if there had been no joint action. The citizens of Mostar progressively gained the confidence to take over responsibility for their own city and thus provided proof that the two communities could live side by side.

Extension of the Non-Proliferation Treaty (NPT)

At first sight non-proliferation was a rather difficult case for the EU with two nuclear and 13 non-nuclear weapon states, with seven countries using more or less extensively nuclear energy and eight that do not, indeed some very much opposed to this form of electricity production. Shared interests were not immediately apparent but in spite of this the EU decided to launch a joint action in support of an extension of the NPT in 1994.

The idea for a joint action on the NPT was first proposed by the Belgian Presidency in October 1993 but did not win immediate approval. In particular, Britain and France feared that they could be pressured to take positions not compatible with their national interests. When the Greek Presidency started in January 1994, the best that could be agreed on was to work on a joint declaration. However, new Greek and German initiatives led to agreement on guidelines for a common preparation of the 1995 NPT Review and Extension Conference in the form of a joint action.

At the 1994 European Council meeting in Corfu, the EU agreed 'to strengthen the international non-proliferation system by promoting the universality of the Treaty on the Non-Proliferation of Nuclear Weapons (NPT) and by extending it indefinitely and unconditionally'. Immediately after the summit, the Council working group (CONUC) met in special session to work out details which were communicated to the Political Committee and then adopted by the Council on 18 July 1994. According to their conclusions, the joint action would consist of:

- an appeal to all parties to participate in the last two Preparatory Committees (Prepcom) of the Review and Extension Conference;
- a campaign to convince bystanders to join the Treaty, a particularly useful move in the case of Algeria;
- a call on all parties to participate in the 1995 Conference;
- and an effort to convince all parties that indefinite extension was the best choice available.

The main diplomatic instrument chosen was the diplomatic démarche to be conducted by the troika and by individual Member States. The EU campaign was conducted in a different style from the occasionally very heavy-handed approach of US diplomacy. The Europeans restricted themselves to exposing the full range of their arguments favouring an unlimited extension of the Treaty, and drawing attention to conditions which would make it impossible to reach this decision and weaken the NPT. While they made it clear that they had a strong interest in the matter they consciously refrained from pressurizing or arm-twisting their interlocutors. They also tended to dismiss the prevailing US strategy to achieve the objective of '50% plus 1' votes for indefinite extension as too small a majority on which to base such a fateful decision. Rather, they attempted to convince as many countries as possible in order to base the decision on near consensus.

Germany in its role of Presidency played an important part in pushing the joint action. At the UN General Assembly the EU memorandum accompanying Foreign Minister Kinkel's statement declared that 'the European Union is in favour of a complete, universal and internationally verifiable test ban treaty'.[10] The first démarche and the result of the Prepcom were evaluated by the Presidency, and, based on this assessment, a second effort was prepared for November 1994. This time, the approach was differentiated: non-participants were called upon to take part in the last Prepcom and the Conference itself; non-members of the NPT (with particular emphasis on Ukraine, Algeria, Argentina and Chile) were invited to accede; known opponents of indefinite extension were approached to convince them of the virtues of the European stance. As a consequence of a Council decision in

10. Statement on behalf of the European Union by the head of Delegation of the Federal Republic of Germany, Ambassador Wolfgang Hoffmann, to the Preparatory Committee for the 1995 Conference of the Parties to the Treaty on the Non-Proliferation of Nuclear Weapons, Third Session, Geneva, 12 September 1994.

October 1994, the doyen of the diplomats of the six Central European states associated with the EU—Poland, Hungary, the Czech Republic, Slovakia, Bulgaria and Romania—accompanied the troika on these démarches. The briefs for the European démarches were all prepared and agreed jointly, so that all would not only aim at the same objective, but also follow the same line of argument. The selection of countries to be approached was also jointly agreed.

Table 4.1: Council Decision of 25 July 1994 (94/509/CFSP) concerning the joint action regarding preparation for the 1995 Conference of the States parties to the Treaty on Non-Proliferation of Nuclear Weapons (excerpts)

Article 1: The objective of this joint action which is the subject of this decision shall be to strengthen the international nuclear non-proliferation system by promoting the universality of the Treaty on the Non-Proliferation of Nuclear Weapons and by extending it indefinitely and unconditionally; Article 2: For the purposes of the objective laid down in Article 1, the European Union shall: – make efforts to convince States which are not yet parties to the Non-Proliferation Treaty to accede, if possible before 1995, and to assist States ready to accede in accelerating their accession; – encourage participation in the remaining two Preparatory Committee sessions of the 1995 Conference of the States parties to the said Treaty in Geneva and New York respectively and in the Conference itself; – help build consensus on the aim of indefinite and unconditional extension of the said Treaty.	Article 3: Action by the European Union as referred to in Article 2 shall comprise: – démarches by the Presidency under the conditions laid down in Article 15 (3) of the Treaty on European Union, with regard to non-member States which are not yet parties to the Non-Proliferation Treaty; – démarches by the Presidency, under the conditions laid down in Article 15 (3) of the Treaty on European Union, with regard to non-member States which might not share the Union's belief that the Non-Proliferation Treaty should be extended indefinitely and unconditionally; – the possibility of assistance by the European Union for non-member States which so wish with a view to their accession to the Non-Proliferation Treaty and the establishment of the procedures necessary for compliance with obligations under it.

The French Presidency continued to press in the same direction: a joint statement for the fourth Prepcom was prepared. Repeated démarches were conducted by the troika, most notably in the Middle East. The Presidency addressed several international conferences on behalf of the Union, for example the meeting of OPANAL, the Latin

American organization for the peaceful use of nuclear energy, to argue for indefinite extension. President Mitterrand of France wrote personally to a number of heads of state and government, explaining the Union's position on the extension question. In parallel to the Presidency's activities, in the last three months before the Conference, Member States were mandated to complete the diplomatic campaign by individual efforts, each using the joint briefs in its activities. This campaign was conducted with a sensible division of labour, assigning approaches to particular countries to Member States with the most 'special relationship' to the party concerned. France, for example, made enormous efforts to talk to each francophone African State with a view to convincing its leadership of the merits of indefinite extension. Spain sent missions to its Latin American partners with the Spanish–Argentinian and Spanish–Peruvian talks proving to be particularly successful. German diplomats visited some of the more difficult places like Mexico City, Caracas, Djakarta and Teheran, in addition to Santiago and Colombo.

The NPT joint action demonstrated that there was considerable common ground, despite the structural and ideological divisions on nuclear policy, on which it was possible to conduct a solid body of common policy. The joint action was a considerable success, in that it combined the efforts of Member States toward a common goal, provoked activities that would otherwise most likely not have been undertaken, and made a discernible, significant contribution to the successful extension outcome. The joint action extended through four presidencies—Belgium, Greece, Germany and France—and demonstrated that continuity was possible despite the obvious difficulties of the rotating Presidency.

Assessment

These three examples of the EU's first joint actions demonstrate that quiet diplomacy can have an impact on different foreign policy issues. The joint actions received very little media coverage but nevertheless made an important contribution to the resolution of difficult and sensitive problems. The EU was able to secure a broad policy consensus on each issue and then followed up with firm diplomatic action. But these quiet diplomatic successes were overshadowed by the continuing fighting in former Yugoslavia and there was a widespread public perception that despite the new CFSP structures, the EU was still not bringing its collective influence to bear decisively on foreign and security policy issues. It was under these difficult circumstances, therefore, that negotiators met in the IGC to discuss improvements to the CFSP machinery.

5 |

The Treaty of Amsterdam

During the first three years of operation there was broad agreement that the CFSP had not lived up to expectations, particularly the 'failure' to bring an early end of the fighting in Yugoslavia. The discussion on the reform of the CFSP began almost before the ink was dry on the TEU. Because of disagreement about the arrangements for CFSP, it was agreed to review the operation of the CFSP during the 1996 IGC. To prepare the groundwork for the IGC, the European Council decided to establish a Reflection Group under the chairmanship of Carlos Westendorp, the State Secretary in the Spanish Ministry of Foreign Affairs, to examine the options for reform. However, as one of the participants wryly remarked, the very name was a misnomer—there was little evidence of reflection and an absence of group dynamics.

The Westendorp Report underlined the importance of the challenge put to the IGC by the perspective of a further enlargement of the Union. It stated that

> enlargement will undoubtedly make for political stability and security for the people of Europe but it will bring a qualitative change to the internal and external dimension of the Union and that therefore preparations must be accomplished inter alia by clarifying the objectives and strengthening the instruments of the Union's external action.[1]

Following the publication of the Westendorp Report, many of the same representatives who had participated in the preparation of the report continued under a new guise, as personal representatives of Member States in the IGC. Both the Italian and Irish Presidencies continued the negotiating and drafting on the basis of the Westendorp report, as well as a multitude of submissions from all Member States,

---

1. For details of the Westendorp Report and other submissions to the IGC see the Europa Server (http://europa.eu.int/en/agenda/igc.html. See also Keatinge (1996).

the Commission, the Council Secretariat, the European Parliament, and a host of non-governmental organizations. This was in marked contrast to the Maastricht negotiations that had been held largely behind closed doors.

The IGC provided a clear indication of the wide divergences of viewpoints between Member States, the European Parliament and the Commission on CFSP questions. Although it was generally agreed that something needed to be done to improve CFSP, there were many opposing opinions as to how these objectives were to be pursued. Thus, some countries advocated the WEU's gradual integration into the EU whereas others did not; some favoured more use of majority voting in relation to CFSP; some advocated the establishment of a High Representative for CFSP whereas others were opposed to this. The UK and France were the most vociferous in seeking to maintain the intergovernmental character of CFSP while Germany, supported by Belgium and Greece, argued that the pillars should be dropped.

Despite French and German differences, they did produce a joint letter before the Dublin European Council in December 1996 which signalled a readiness both to compromise and to move forward in the CFSP field. The letter stated that there should be a face for the CFSP who should 'take charge of the CFSP'. He would have the necessary 'political qualification', and would take part in meetings of all relevant EU bodies. Mr CFSP would pursue his mandates 'in close cooperation with the Presidency and the Commissioner in charge of foreign relations'. QMV should become the general rule while constructive abstention was also proposed. The letter also suggested that the European Council should play a more important role in defining priorities for the Union; and should also set policy guidelines for the WEU, which should be integrated into the Union according to a timetable.

As far as the Commission was concerned, it had never disguised its dislike of the pillar structure agreed at Maastricht. In its submission to the IGC in February 1996, the Commission stated that the EU had failed 'to assert its identity on the international scene' and therefore the IGC should have a clear and simple aim—to empower the Union 'to act rather than react'. The Commission proposed that the prime objectives of the IGC in external relations should be: to bring together the various strands comprising foreign relations into a single effective whole, with structures and procedures designed to enhance consistency and continuity; to improve the common foreign and security policy at all stages of its operation; and to establish a proper European identity with regard to security and defence, as an integral part of the common foreign and security policy. The Commission stated that the Union's external policy as a whole would not be effective until there was proper coordination between its various components. The Treaty already required the Council and the Commission to pursue a consistent foreign policy, but this had not happened under the Treaty as it stood, and the institutions' duties in this respect should thus be reinforced.

While recognizing that the essential point was for Member States to demonstrate the necessary political will to make the CFSP work effectively, the Commission proposed a number of measures to improve all stages of CFSP procedures. As regards the preparation of decisions, the Commission argued that a 'joint analysis unit' should be created, composed of experts from the Member States and the Commission which would be a joint service of the Council and Commission. The Commission also considered that the formulation of foreign policy would be facilitated by the incorporation of a permanent Political Committee into the Council's existing machinery for preparing decisions in Brussels. The Commission favoured constructive abstention and proposed that QMV should be the norm for the CFSP with unanimity being retained only for decisions involving military matters.

Primary responsibility for implementation of the CFSP should lie with the Presidency and the Commission. However, this clearly should not prevent certain tasks being allocated to specific personalities (special envoys) designated on an ad hoc basis. The Commission also called for expenditure incurred in implementing the common foreign and security policy to be included in the Community budget, unless an express decision to the contrary was taken.

On the security and defence front, the Commission stated that the CFSP had suffered as a result of its inability to project credible military force. While NATO would remain at the centre of Europe's defence arrangements for the foreseeable future, a European pillar based on the WEU should be developed within the alliance. Accordingly, the IGC should agree that the Union should take responsibility for the 'Petersberg tasks', that is, providing for peacekeeping and peace enforcement missions; hold regular meetings of Defence Ministers; and incorporate the WEU into the Union according to an agreed timetable.

Finally, the Commission recalled that the security and defence of the Union was dependent on the existence of a solid industrial base, which meant that there should be better integration of the armaments industry into the general Treaty rules, and greater solidarity and cooperation, including the establishment of an armaments agency.[2]

The Commission's contribution was generally well received by most Member States. Some considered it had been too timid, others that it had been too ambitious. Interestingly its views were broadly in line with those of the European Parliament.

In December 1996, the Irish Presidency tabled a draft text of treaty changes which sought to synthesize the discussion in the IGC and present a number of options for CFSP reform. The draft suggested a reinforcement of Article C to ensure that the Council and Commission cooperated more effectively to ensure greater policy consistency. The draft also proposed a strengthened strategic guidance role for the European Council. The most interesting innovation was the concept of a new troika involving the Presidency, the Secretary General of the Council (Mr CFSP) and the Commission. The old troika would thus disappear although the incoming Presidency could be called upon when appropriate. The draft also retained the option of the Union appointing special representatives. The various actors in the new troika all had a role at each phase of the CFSP process and hence there would have to be greater emphasis on coordination.

A declaration was suggested for the new planning staff which would be situated in the Council. Its exact mandate, role and staffing remained to be decided. The draft proposed that joint actions should be made by unanimity but with the possibility of constructive abstention (and non-participation). Decisions about common positions could, however, be made by qualified majority.[3]

As regards security and defence, the Presidency text was an improvement on previous texts by eliminating certain ambiguities and simplifying certain provisions. In general, the Presidency found a judicious balance but did not pronounce directly on two significant questions: (1) a timetable for the integration of the WEU; and (2) an optional protocol for mutual defence. At the IGC much time had been spent debating the

---

2.   See the Commission submission to the IGC in February 1996—available on the Europa server (see n. 1).

3.   The Irish Presidency draft text was entitled 'An Effective and Coherent Foreign Policy'—the clear implication being that the CFSP was ineffective and incoherent!

relationship between the EU and WEU. The Presidency suggested that 'the Union will avail itself of the WEU', which was a new formula.

The final stages of the IGC produced a broad consensus on the CFSP, albeit partly as a result of exhaustion and partly from a recognition that some countries had drawn clear 'lines in the sand'. Some States, and the Commission, would have preferred a bolder text, but given the need for unanimity, it was not possible to secure more far-reaching changes.

The Amsterdam Treaty[4]

In terms of consistency, the pillar structure of the Maastricht Treaty was not affected, although a substantial part of the policies falling in the third pillar were subject to community procedures. Nevertheless, the new treaty recognized an increased need for consistency in external relations. Article 3 was amended to stress the duty of both the Council and the Commission to cooperate to ensure consistency. The new Article 14 para. 4 states that the Council may request the Commission to submit proposals on CFSP to ensure the implementation of a joint action. The Declaration on the new planning unit explicitly states that appropriate cooperation with the Commission shall be established in order to ensure full coherence.

Article 11 has added a new CFSP objective: the safeguard of the 'integrity of the Union in conformity with the principles of the UN Charter'. The significance of the inclusion of phrase 'integrity of the Union' is not, however, obvious and no guidance is provided as to what the 'Union's integrity' means or how or by whom this integrity may be threatened. The same article introduces a new obligation for Member States who 'shall work together to enhance and develop their mutual political solidarity'.

The new treaty clarified the distinction between joint actions and common positions and introduced a new instrument (common strategies) without defining it clearly. Article 12 lists the CFSP instruments as: principles and general guidelines; common strategies; joint actions; common positions and systematic cooperation. Article 13 specifies that principles/general guidelines and common strategies are defined by the European Council. Common strategies are to be adopted in areas where Member States have important interests in common. Article 14 defines joint actions saying that they shall address specific situations where

4.   The full text of Article V is given in Appendix 1.

operational action is needed. Article 15 defines common positions as 'defining the approach of the Union to a particular matter of a geographical or thematic nature'.[5]

The Treaty reinforces the role of the European Council (Art. 13) and brings a new actor into CFSP—the Secretary General of the Council (Mr CFSP). He will act as the High Representative for CFSP (Art. 18 para. 3), will assist the Council in CFSP matters, in particular conducting political dialogue with third parties (Art. 26) and will head the new policy planning and early warning unit. The unit will consist of personnel drawn from the General Secretariat, Member States, the Commission and WEU. Its tasks shall include, among others, 'producing at the request of either the Council or the Presidency or on its own initiative, argued policy options papers to be presented under the responsibility of the Presidency'. Any Member State or the Commission may make suggestions to the unit for work to be undertaken. According to Article 26, the High Representative for the CFSP shall assist the Council in the formulation and preparation of policy decisions.

The Presidency, the Secretary General and the Commission will constitute a new troika. The Commission's role was not modified: it remains 'fully associated' with the CFSP (Art. 27). The Parliament's involvement in CFSP also remains modest: it shall be consulted and informed (Art. 21). In CFSP financing the institutional balance is somewhat different since the Commission and the European Parliament have a more important role to play.

The initiative in the CFSP is still shared between Member States and the Commission (Art. 22). The Treaty of Amsterdam increases the use of QMV in the CFSP but still considers unanimity as the general principle. Article 23 envisages three voting procedures for the Council: unanimity, QMV and a majority of Member States. The principle of unanimity is nuanced by the possibility of constructive abstention. The Member State abstaining will not be obliged to apply the decision but shall accept that the decision commits the Union and shall refrain from any action likely to conflict with EU action. However, if the Member States abstaining constructively represent more than one-third of the votes (weighted according to the QMV rules), the decision will not be adopted. The Council will be able to act by QMV (62 votes in favour cast by at least 10 members) when adopting decisions on the basis of a common strategy (adopted by unanimity by the European Council) or

5.   See the Glossary for fuller details.

decisions implementing a joint action/common position. However, a Member State can oppose the adoption of a decision by QMV for 'important and stated reasons of national policy'. In this case, the Council may, by QMV, refer the matter to the European Council who will decide by unanimity. QMV will not apply to military decisions. The Council will act by a majority of its members for procedural questions.

The new Article 28 states the principle that CFSP operational expenditure shall be charged to the budget of the European Communities and recognizes two exceptions: military operations and when the Council unanimously decides otherwise. If expenditure is not charged to the EC budget, it shall be charged to Member States according to GNP. In case of a military operation decided with the constructive abstention of one or some Member States, these shall not be obliged to contribute to its financing.

An inter-institutional agreement on CFSP financing stated that CFSP expenditure would be non-obligatory, which means that the European Parliament has the last word. It foresees that, on the basis of the Commission's proposal, the European Parliament and the Council shall annually secure agreement on the global amount of CFSP expenditure. This global amount will be allocated among new articles of the CFSP budgetary chapter (i.e. observation of elections, EU envoys, prevention of conflicts, disarmament, international conferences and urgent actions). No funds will be entered into a reserve.

Article 17 was the result of conflicting views of Member States on the most difficult CFSP issue of the IGC negotiations—security and defence. The treaty improvements included:

- a change in the language with the 'eventual' framing of a common defence policy becoming a 'progressive' one (Art. 17 para. 1);
- the 'Petersberg tasks' (humanitarian and rescue tasks, peacekeeping tasks and tasks of combat forces in crisis management, including peacemaking) appearing in the Treaty (Art. 17 para. 2);
- the EU 'will avail itself of the WEU to elaborate and implement decisions of the Union which have defence implications'. When the EU avails itself of the WEU on the Petersberg tasks, all contributing Member States will be able to participate fully and on an equal footing in planning and decision-taking in the WEU (Art. 17 para. 3).

The idea of a draft protocol on the WEU integration into the EU with a specific timetable was finally abandoned. Nevertheless Article 17 para. 1 still considers the WEU as 'an integral part of the development of the Union' and adds the idea that the WEU will provide the Union with access to an operational capability, notably for the 'Petersberg tasks'. In addition the competence of the European Council to establish guidelines in accordance with Article 13 shall also obtain in respect of the WEU for those matters for which the Union avails itself of the WEU (Art. 17 para. 3). According to a Protocol to Article 17, arrangements for enhanced cooperation between the EU and WEU were to be drawn up within a year from the entry into force of this Protocol (see Appendix 2).

In relation to NATO, Article 17 para. 1 says that the policy of the Union 'shall respect the obligations of certain Member States, which see their common defence realized in NATO, under the North Atlantic Treaty'. Cooperation in the field of armaments 'as Member States consider appropriate' is not formulated in very strong terms.

The Amsterdam draft treaty dropped the idea of recognizing the EU as a legal personality. Nevertheless the new Article 24 foresees the possibility of international agreements in CFSP without specifying who will be a party to them. It could be interpreted in the future as recognizing an implicit legal personality for the EU. Such agreements shall be negotiated by the Presidency, 'assisted by the Commission as appropriate' (i.e. not on a regular basis) after authorization by the Council, acting unanimously. They will be concluded by the Council, by unanimity, on a recommendation of the Presidency. A Declaration specifies that this article and the agreements resulting from it shall not imply any transfer of competence from Member States to the Union.

Assessment of the Changes

A constant theme of the IGC was the need to make improvements in the CFSP, not as an end in itself, but in order to defend the interests of the Member States and its citizens. The Union ought to be better able to pursue more effectively the objective already set out in Article B of the Treaty, that is 'to assert its identity on the international scene'. However, translating this general intention into reality, or into clear choices for reform, did not prove to be easy, particularly as the CFSP does not comprise the totality of the Union's external affairs, for alongside this embryonic policy, the Community has long-standing responsibilities for trade, development and humanitarian aid.

Given the differences between the Member States in 1995–96, it is hardly surprising that the Amsterdam Treaty did not fundamentally alter the character of CFSP. The reforms were of an incremental character and designed to make the existing CFSP structures work better. As one participant remarked, it was more like a 10,000-mile service than a new engine. As had been the case at Maastricht, the negotiations on CFSP at Amsterdam proved to be a tortuous exercise in attempting to reconcile the seemingly irreconcilable positions of Member States on a wide range of issues. Moreover, the approaches to CFSP at both Maastricht and Amsterdam were rather insular in that they failed to take adequate account of the potential impact of enlargement upon the Union's decision taking capacities, still less upon the direction and substance of the Union's external relations.

Despite reform of the CFSP being one of the main reasons for holding the IGC, and despite a large measure of agreement on the need to improve its operation, the outcome at Amsterdam was thus rather modest. The main improvements to the CFSP included a strengthened role for the European Council in defining CFSP principles and guidelines (common strategies). There was also provision for the Council and Commission to exercise greater coherence and consistency while the establishment of Mr CFSP and the new planning unit should lead to a greater conceptual capacity, continuity and visibility. Decision-making should become easier with the introduction of QMV and constructive abstention; while the Union now takes on responsibility for all 'Petersberg' security tasks, that is, virtually all tasks except territorial defence.

However, past experience suggests that appropriate structures and procedures alone will not be not enough to ensure a coherent and effective foreign and security policy. There must be the political will to exploit them fully if a real CFSP should emerge. This will require a deeper awareness among Member States of the interests they share as EU members as well as of the fact that even many of their national interests might be served better when pursued jointly. CFSP players on all levels will slowly have to learn to overcome the 'traditions and emotions' of foreign policy described by Walter Hallstein and to look at themselves not only as national representatives but as participants in a common enterprise: the shaping of a genuine European foreign and security policy.

6 |

The Security Dimension

The European security landscape has changed dramatically during the 1990s. There is no longer any threat from a powerful Soviet Red Army but other threats have emerged in a radically altered security environment. For example, there have been a number of ethnic conflicts in the Balkans and instability on other parts of the EU's periphery. NATO has taken in three new former communist countries (Poland, Hungary and the Czech Republic) while the EU is negotiating membership with these and several other countries from Central and Eastern Europe. Both NATO and the EU have established strategic relationships with Russia and Ukraine. Apart from the EU and NATO, other institutions, including the OSCE and WEU, are also changing, leaving European security in a state of flux following the end of the Cold War.

Defining Security

Apart from 'federalism', there are few words used as often as 'security' in international relations, which suggest different meanings to different audiences. Numerous adjectives such as 'military', 'external', 'internal', 'hard' and 'soft', are currently used when discussing security. For the armed forces, security usually has a military connotation. For the citizens in most parts of Europe, security is viewed primarily as freedom from criminal activities. For the planners in foreign ministries and the inhabitants of think tanks, security is conceived in a wider context involving military, political, economic, environmental and other aspects.[1]

It is important to emphasize that the end of the Cold War has brought a significant improvement in terms of European security. However, as the military threat has declined, new more diverse security threats have emerged, some indeed as a legacy of the communist era. Nearly all

1. For discussions about post-Cold War security concepts see Park and Rees (1998).

present-day conflicts are within rather than between States. Among the most serious of these new threats are political and economic instability (e.g. in several Balkan countries), ethnic and border problems (former Yugoslavia, including Kosovo, Chechnya), terrorism, organized crime and environmental degradation. Organized crime, in particular drug trafficking, is much more serious than many issues that have tradition- ally been seen as a threat to national security because it poses a threat to security at three levels: the individual, the state and the international system. Organizations that deal in drugs can also traffic in technology and components for weapons of mass destruction. Whether the recipi- ents of such transfers are terrorist organizations or 'pariah' states, the link between criminal activities and security is obvious. If non-prolif- eration and other regulatory regimes are to function effectively in future, therefore, it will be necessary to curb the activities of organized crime. This will not be easy.

Tackling many of the environmental threats, which have often arisen as a result of years of communist neglect will also not be easy. All over the former Soviet Union the degradation of the environment is dramatic and can have security implications. If used by political leaders to mobi- lize groups through appeals to group identity, disputes over land, water and other natural resources could quickly lead to a radicalization of those groups, with disruptive effects on the political process. In the Fergana Valley with its 14 million inhabitants, where Uzbekistan, Taji- kistan and Kyrgystan border on each other, the struggle for sufficient land and water has already led to violent conflict.

States are reasonably well equipped to deal with traditional security threats from other countries, but when they are faced with sovereignty- free actors they are unsure which instruments and strategies are appro- priate. Most governments have yet to acknowledge the scale and com- plexity of the new threats, let alone engage in more extensive functional cooperation arrangements with each other. Existing security arrange- ments are based on legal commitments undertaken by States reputed to be 'sovereign'. In a world of ever-increasing interdependence and per- meability of national boundaries the relevance of national sovereignty in dealing with the complexity of today's problems is doubtful.[2]

Equally no one State can deal with the problems that characterize the regions on Europe's periphery. For example, the problems on the southern shores of the Mediterranean are immense: high unemploy-

2.   See Kirchner and Sperling (1996) and Waever *et al.* (1993).

ment, low economic growth, high debts, low exports, poor infrastructure, degradation of the environment—all fuelled by a population explosion resulting in an age structure in which 50% of the population is under 15. This is a potentially explosive situation with obvious implications for European security. EU policy, including assistance, to the region is far more effective if carried out by the 15 acting together, as in the Euro-Mediterranean (Barcelona) Process, rather than on an individual basis. The growing willingness of the EU to work together on such security issues is shown by the change in the agendas of meetings of EU Foreign Ministers. While 10 years ago they spent most of their time discussing political-military issues, today the emphasis is on trade agreements, technical assistance, sanctions, closing down unsafe nuclear reactors, balance of payments support, humanitarian aid and similar issues.

Another concept that requires fresh thinking is the role of the military. During the Cold War security was largely seen in terms of military power. The Soviet Union built up a huge military apparatus but arguably the resources which the military consumed helped to destroy rather than protect the Soviet system. A large military power not underpinned by a healthy economy is a threat in itself. Military power will remain an important asset in support of diplomatic efforts (e.g. Iraq, Bosnia, Kosovo) but military power alone cannot solve the myriad of new security problems facing Europe. The emphasis must be on preventing conflicts arising in the first place. This is indeed one of the main tasks of armed forces today and there is a considerable need to increase public awareness, and multi-national training for conflict prevention. Civilian forces also need to be prepared. The glaring deficiency in Bosnia and Kosovo was less well-armed and well-trained armed forces than trained police, local government and other civilian officials.

The Institutional Maze

Given the nature of the above problems, it makes sense for the many institutions involved with security issues to engage in the closest possible cooperation. It is sometimes bewildering to contemplate the alphabet soup of institutions—the UN, EU, WEU, NATO, EAPC, OSCE, G7/8, Contact Group—involved in European security. However, each of these institutions contributes something distinctive and useful to the overall security in Europe and there are substantial synergistic benefits from cooperation between them.

Table 6.1: The European security architecture

	OSCE	NATO	EAPC	EU	WEU[a]	CE
Albania	✓	–	✓	–	–	✓
Andorra	✓	–	–	–	–	✓
Armenia	✓	–	✓	–	–	✓
Austria	✓	✓	–	✓	O	✓
Azerbaizan	✓	–	✓	–	–	✓
Belarus	✓	–	✓	–	–	✓
Belgium	✓	✓	✓	✓	FM	✓
Bosnia-H.	✓	–	–	–	–	–
Bulgaria	✓	✓	✓	–	AP	–
Canada	✓	✓	✓	–	–	–
Croatia	✓	–	–	–	–	✓
Cyprus	✓	–	–	–	–	✓
Czech Rep.	✓	✓	✓	–	AM	✓
Denmark	–	✓	✓	✓	O	–
Estonia	✓	✓	✓	–	AP	–
Finland	✓	✓	–	✓	O	✓
France	✓	✓	✓	✓	FM	✓
Georgia	✓	–	✓	–	–	✓
Germany	✓	✓	✓	✓	FM	✓
Greece	✓	✓	✓	✓	FM	✓
Hungary	✓	✓	✓	–	AM	✓
Iceland	✓	✓	✓	–	AM	✓
Ireland	✓	✓	✓	✓	O	✓
Italy	✓	✓	✓	✓	FM	✓
Kazakhstan	✓	–	✓	–	–	✓
Krygyzstan	✓	–	✓	–	–	✓
Latvia	✓	✓	✓	–	AP	–
Liechtenstein	✓	–	–	–	–	✓
Lithuania	✓	✓	✓	–	AP	–
Luxembourg	✓	✓	✓	✓	FM	✓
Macedonia	✓	–	–	–	–	✓
Malta	✓	–	–	–	–	✓
Moldova	✓	✓	–	–	–	✓
Monaco	✓	–	–	–	–	–
Netherlands	✓	✓	✓	✓	FM	✓
Norway	✓	✓	✓	–	AM	✓
Poland	✓	✓	✓	–	AM	✓
Portugal	✓	✓	✓	✓	FM	✓
Romania	✓	✓	✓	–	AP	–
Russia	✓	✓	–	–	–	✓
San Marino	✓	–	–	–	–	✓
Slovakia	✓	✓	✓	–	AP	–
Slovenia	✓	✓	✓	–	AP	–
Spain	✓	✓	✓	✓	FM	✓
Sweden	✓	✓	–	✓	O	✓
Switzerland	✓	–	–	–	–	✓
Tajikistan	✓	–	✓	–	–	✓
Turkey	✓	✓	✓	–	AM	✓
Turkmenistan	✓	–	✓	–	–	✓
UK	✓	✓	✓	✓	FM	✓
Ukraine	✓	✓	–	–	–	✓
US	✓	✓	✓	–	–	–
Uzbekistan	✓	–	✓	–	–	✓
Vatican City	✓	–	–	–	–	–
Yug. Fed.[b]	✓	–	–	–	–	–

[a] FM: Full Members; O: Observers; AM: Associate Members; AP: Associate Partners
[b] Suspended from action.

In the still emerging security architecture in post-Cold War Europe, security is centred on cooperation not confrontation or division into blocs. These security networks help to avoid a 'we' and 'they' syndrome which could be both divisive and dangerous. The OSCE, with 55 members, is the most comprehensive. It is organized on intergovernmental lines and takes decisions by consensus. In recent years it has become more and more involved in conflict prevention and resolution. Its presence in many conflict zones, including Chechnya, Albania, Bosnia, Moldova, Tajikistan, Nagorno Karabakh and Kosovo has been positive. It has sought to develop a 'European Security Model' and a 'European Security Charter'.[3] The EU cooperates with the OSCE through fact-finding missions and in monitoring and humanitarian missions. But the OSCE effort is limited by its small budget and small permanent staff—less than 100 officials.

The Council of Europe, with 40 members, contributes to the preservation and safeguarding of the values of democracy and human rights. Its high membership standards, technical assistance to support the reform of legal systems, and monitoring missions play an important role in exporting security to countries in transition. But it also suffers from scarce budgetary and human resources.

Like the EU, the Atlantic Alliance—NATO—is in the process of internal transformation and enlargement. The Washington summit in April 1999, the fiftieth anniversary of NATO, saw Poland, Hungary and the Czech Republic sitting at the table as full members, while the queue to join grew longer. To appease those waiting, NATO developed a network of relationships with non-members, through its Partnership for Peace Programmes and through the Euro Atlantic Partnership Council.[4]

NATO has also become involved in military operations for the first time since it was established in 1949. NATO (mainly US) aircraft bombed Serbian targets in 1995 to help bring Milosovic to the negotiating table, organized and controlled the policing of the Dayton Agreement through SFOR and then launched a major attack on Serbia in the spring of 1999 in order to secure Yugoslav compliance with international arrangements for the future of Kosovo.

NATO enlargement and the NATO campaign against the Serbs in

---

3. A report on the European Security model can be found at http://www. osceprag.cz/info/facts/1s96ew02.htm

4. Documents approved at the Washington summit may be found on www. nato.int/docu/pr/1999

Kosovo were bitterly opposed by Russia who saw its own security and influence under threat. Partly to assuage Russian feeling, NATO and Russia signed in May 1997 a charter establishing a Joint Permanent Council that has a wide mandate to discuss European security issues. A similar charter was signed with Ukraine in July 1997. NATO also made clear that it did not intend to station nuclear weapons or construct new military bases on the territory of the new Member States. Since 1997 Russia has been more preoccupied with domestic than external problems, and has adopted a pragmatic approach to cooperation with NATO forces in Bosnia. But this cooperation was severely tested as a result of the NATO bombing of Serbia and Russia proved a tough negotiating partner in the division of command arrangements for the international peacekeeping force (KFOR) in Kosovo.

The Defence Dimension

Until recently, the security and defence dimension of the CFSP has always been an area of considerable disagreement between the Member States. Disputes covered fundamental issues such as whether the EU should strive for a defence dimension and what might be the implications for NATO if it did. Although a majority of EU members are also members of the WEU, the WEU is not yet a European Union institution, despite various EU declarations concerning the close relationship between the two organizations. Only 10 out of 15 EU countries are full members. The other five have observer status. A total of 28 countries formally participate in the WEU as full members, 'observers', 'associate members' or 'associated partners' (see Appendix 3).

The WEU's 'full members' list is, in 1999, the UK, France, Germany, Italy, Spain, Portugal, Belgium, the Netherlands, Luxembourg and Greece. Denmark and Ireland became observers in 1992 and Austria, Finland and Sweden in 1995. Norway, Iceland, Turkey, Hungary, Poland and the Czech Republic, the six European states which are NATO members but not EU members, are 'associate members'. Seven Central and East European countries have the 'associate partner' status accorded at Luxembourg in May 1994. Observers are allowed to attend WEU Council meetings and are invited to working-group meetings where on request they may be allowed to speak. Associate members may take a part in Council meetings and working groups. They may also associate themselves with the decisions of

Member States and can also participate in military operations by the WEU. Neither associate member nor associate partner status includes security guarantees. The attraction of associate membership of the WEU still lies primarily in its connection to the EU rather than the intrinsic merits of this organization.

Dormant for many years, the WEU awoke in the 1990s and was given a number of modest tasks. It found that its main role had changed from collective defence to crisis management (e.g. sanctions monitoring), peace support (e.g. training police forces) and humanitarian missions. The WEU can carry out missions when requested to do so by the EU, the UN, OSCE and WEU member countries. In June 1992, the foreign and defence ministers of the WEU met in Petersberg (near Bonn) in order to define the role and tasks of the WEU. This resulted in the 'Petersberg Declaration', outlining the guidelines for the WEU's future development. The declaration re-affirmed NATO's responsibility for collective self-defence and defined its own roles as those of peace-making, peacekeeping, crisis management and protection for humanitarian operations. These Petersberg tasks are included in the Treaty of Amsterdam.

There has always been a question mark over WEU's credibility. Dwarfed by NATO, the WEU's clearest weakness has been its inability to carve out for itself a distinct purpose. Like NATO, the WEU has no forces of its own but unlike NATO it has no permanent command structures. But in the 1990s it began to develop some modest capabilities and experience. For example, it has a Planning Cell, a Satellite Centre and a Military Committee (consisting of the Chiefs of Defence staff) to facilitate performance of its 'Petersberg tasks'. It also has 'Forces Answerable to WEU' (FAWEU) which comprise national units plus several multinational formations. The multinational FAWEU currently comprise of the Eurocorps (Germany, France, Belgium, Luxembourg and Spain).

The operational command of Eurocorps Divisions remains under each national authority. The Eurocorps was declared operational in November 1995 and has its headquarters located in Strasbourg. There are a number of other multinational forces including the Multinational Division Centre (MNDC) (Germany, Belgium, Holland, and the UK); EUROFOR (Rapid Deployment Force) (France, Italy, Portugal and Spain); EUROMARFOR (European Maritime Force) (France, Italy, Portugal and Spain); the headquarters of the First German–Netherlands

Corps; and the Spanish–Italian Amphibious Force. The Joint Arma-ments Cooperation Structure (OCCAR) established in 1996 may lead to a European armaments agency and may at some point be brought within the WEU. These multinational formations are indicative of a desire for closer cooperation in defence between groups of Member States within the Union. They provide useful additional experience of cooperation and may help to facilitate the emergence of a common European defence culture.[5]

A substantial degree of cooperation between the WEU and NATO is developing. In 1994, a NATO summit called for a European Security and Defence Identity (ESDI) involving both organizations. A formula for ESDI was adopted by NATO foreign ministers in Berlin in June 1996 and was further elaborated at a NATO summit meeting in July 1997, involving the strengthening of institutional cooperation between the WEU and NATO. It provides for NATO's full support for ESDI within NATO, through allowing NATO's assets and capabilities to be made available for WEU operations, on a case-by-case basis. ESDI within NATO is based on the idea of separable but not separate capabilities.

Ideas are being developed for combined joint task forces (CJTFs), involving both NATO and WEU military capabilities. The Council of the WEU and the North Atlantic Council agreed to combined opera-tions, including a single commander for the NATO/WEU task force for the enforcement of the embargo in the Adriatic. A network of cross-participation in NATO and WEU committees has also been developed. There are also provisions for European command arrangements within a future new command structure for WEU operations; the creation of forces able to operate under the political guidance and strategic direc-tion of the WEU; arrangements for identifying NATO assets and capa-bilities to support WEU-led operations; joint consultations between NATO and the WEU in crisis management; involvement of the WEU in NATO's defence planning; and plans for joint exercises.[6]

From St Malo to Cologne

The debate on a common defence policy of the European Union was given a considerable boost in the latter half of 1998 when a significant

---

5.   For details of the strength of the armed forces in each Member State of the Union, and each candidate country, see Appendix 6.

6.   For further details see http://www.weu.int/eng/welcome.html

change of British policy led to the Franco–British Declaration on European Defence in St Malo. Prime Minister Blair had raised the need for the EU to have a defence role at the informal European Council in Pörtschach in October 1998 and the Austrians followed up a month later by hosting the first ever informal EU defence ministers meeting and also arranging a meeting between the Austrian Presidency and the Secretary General of NATO. The thrust of all this activity was a consensus on the need to make European security policy and crisis management more effective and efficient.

A number of key issues were identified. First, the question of EU/WEU operational requirements in terms of workable and flexible command structures, suitably equipped and trained forces, and strategic assets such as intelligence and transport capacities. Secondly, the industrial base to develop a competitive European armaments market. Thirdly, the appropriate institutions and procedures for a European defence policy.

In the Amsterdam Treaty the Member States agreed (Art. 17) that the CFSP 'shall include all questions relating to the security of the Union, including the progressive framing of a common defence policy, which might lead to a common defence, should the European Council so decide…' It also agreed that the Union

> shall foster closer institutional relations with the WEU with a view to the possibility of the integration of the WEU into the Union, should the European Council so decide… The progressive framing of a common defence policy will be supported, as Member States consider appropriate, by co-operation between them in the field of armaments. Questions referred to in this Article shall include humanitarian and rescue tasks, peace-keeping tasks and tasks of combat forces in crisis management, including peacemaking. The Union will avail itself of the WEU to elaborate and implement decisions and actions of the Union which have defence implications.

In the Protocol to Article 17, Member States agreed to draw up, within a year from the entry into force of the Treaty of Amsterdam, arrangements for enhanced cooperation between the EU and WEU.[7] Even before the new Treaty entered into force, there were numerous measures taken to strengthen ties between the EU and WEU, including joint meetings of the relevant bodies of both organizations, the harmonization of the sequence of Presidencies as far as possible from 1999

7.   See Appendix 2.

onwards, greater exchange of information between both organizations, joint working groups and a modus operandi for linking the decision-making between the EU and WEU in crisis situations.

At the informal Pörtschach summit, Tony Blair stated that the current situation in European foreign and security policy was 'unacceptable' and marked by 'weakness and confusion', notably with a view to the experience made in Bosnia and Kosovo. He called for a greater EU effort while avoiding setting out any blueprint for institutional change. A few weeks later Britain and France issued a 'Joint Declaration on European Defence' at their bilateral meeting in St Malo. The Heads of State and Government of both countries agreed that:

> It will be important to achieve full and rapid implementation of the Amsterdam provisions on CFSP. This includes the responsibility of the European Council to decide on the progressive framing of a common defence policy in the framework of CFSP. The Council must be able to take decisions on an intergovernmental basis, covering the whole range of activity set out in Title V of the Treaty on European Union.
>
> To this end, the Union must have the capacity for autonomous action, backed up by credible military forces, the means to decide to use them, and a readiness to do so, in order to respond to international crises. In pursuing our objective, the collective defence commitments...must be maintained... Europeans will operate within the institutional framework of the European Union (European Council, General Affairs Council, and meetings of defence ministers).
>
> In order for the European Union to take decisions and approve military action where the Alliance as a whole is not engaged, the Union must be given appropriate structures and a capacity for analysis of situations, sources of intelligence, and a capability for relevant strategic planning, without unnecessary duplication, taking account of the existing assets of the WEU and the evolution of its relations with the EU. In this regard, the European Union will also need to have recourse to suitable military means (European capabilities – pre-designated within NATO's European pillar or national or multinational European means outside the NATO framework).
>
> Europe needs strengthened armed forces that can react rapidly to the new risks, and which are supported by a strong and competitive European defence industry and technology...[8]

The St Malo Declaration was endorsed by the European Council in Vienna in December 1998. The Heads of State and Government also welcomed the intention of the WEU to conduct an audit of the assets

8.   *Agence Europe*, 6 December 1998.

available for European operations and urged the completion of arrangements for enhanced cooperation between the EU and WEU so that these could come into effect on the Treaty's entry into force.

Receiving the Charlemagne Award in Aix-la-Chapelle on 13 May 1999, British Prime Minister Tony Blair spoke, among other things, of the prospects for a European defence policy, declaring:

> When we began the European defence debate at Pörtschach in Austria and then followed it with the St Malo Declaration, there was rightly a sense of optimism. It was a breakthrough. But is only a start. There is much talk of structures. But we should begin with capabilities. To put it bluntly, if Europe is to have a key defence role, it needs modern forces, strategic lift, and the necessary equipment to conduct a campaign. No nation will ever yield up its sovereign right to determine the use of its own armed forces. We do, however, need to see how we can co-operate better, complement each other's capability, have a full range of defence options open to us. This also means greater integration in the defence industry and procurement. If we were in any doubts about this before, Kosovo should have removed them.[9]

The Cologne European Council of 3–4 June 1999 marked a decisive step forward in the development of a Common Security and Defence Policy. Although the Heads of State and Government postponed a formal decision on the institutional issues involved until the end of 2000 a consensus emerged on giving the Union a stronger role in international affairs through a strengthened CFSP backed up by credible military forces and appropriate institutional decision-making structures.

As far as the institutional aspects are concerned, European leaders expressed their will to include defence policy structures into the EU's CFSP pillar, whereby alternative options such as developing the autonomy of WEU, the exclusive focus on ESDI within NATO or the establishment of a fourth pillar within the EU were dismissed. Member States agreed that the EU Council will make decisions on military crisis management by consensus/unanimity with opt-out rights for Member States who do not wish to participate (Petersberg formula). In order to have the appropriate mechanisms for decisions on crisis management and to secure the political control and strategic direction of EU crisis management operations Member States agreed to set up:

- regular (or ad hoc) meetings of the General Affairs Council, as appropriate including Defence Ministers;

9. *Agence Europe*, 14 May 1999.

- a permanent body in Brussels (Political and Security Committee) consisting of representatives with political and military expertise;
- an EU Military Committee consisting of Military Representatives making recommendations to the Political and Security Committee;
- an EU Military Staff including a Situation Centre;
- other resources such as a Satellite Centre and Institute for Security Studies.

The European Council also confirmed that all EU members would have the right to participate on an 'equal footing' in EU operations and that 'satisfactory arrangements' will be worked out for non-EU European NATO allies and for associate partners. Moreover they expressed their will that the EU should have the capability for 'autonomous action' by drawing on national or multinational European command structures and forces (such as the EUROCORPS) or for action by recourse to NATO assets and capabilities. As far as NATO is concerned, arrangements should be found to assure EU access to NATO planning and the availability of 'pre-defined' NATO capabilities for EU-led operations.

This breakthrough in the debate on a European defence policy came about because of the coincidence of a number of factors: the experience of Europe's military weakness in the Kosovo crisis which made all governments convinced of the need to develop an EU crisis management capacity; the fundamental change of British policy; and the supportive attitude of the United States. The Washington NATO summit communiqué 'welcomed the new impetus given to the strengthening of a common European policy in security and defence and confirmed that a stronger European role would contribute to the vitality of the Alliance'.[10]

The debate before Cologne was mainly centred around three controversial issues:

- whether the WEU should be merged with the EU as provided for as a possibility in Article 17 of the TEU;
- whether Article V of the WEU Treaty should be maintained inside or outside the EU framework;
- whether at Cologne or at a later date a formal decision should be taken by the European Council to set up a Common European Defence Policy.

10. See NATO's web site for full details of the Washington summit.

The German Presidency, in line with traditional German thinking on WEU, was very much in favour of merging WEU with the EU and doing so earlier rather than later. This met with opposition on the part of the neutral and non-aligned countries but also on the part of France. The neutral and non-aligned countries (Austria, Sweden, Finland and Ireland) feared that integrating WEU fully into the EU would mean acceptance of a mutual defence commitment that would be difficult to sell to their respective domestic audiences. France feared that transferring the WEU too quickly into the EU would lead to a watering down of the WEU acquis including the collective defence commitment.

The Cologne summit declaration did not speak of the integration of the WEU into the EU, but of the 'inclusion' into the EU 'of those functions of the WEU which will be necessary for the EU to fulfil its new responsibilities in the area of the Petersberg tasks'. The formal decisions should be taken 'by the end of the year 2000 whereby the WEU as an organisation would have completed its purpose'.

On the whole, the agreements of the Cologne summit mark a milestone in the development of the European defence policy—a process that would have been unthinkable a few years ago. However, there remains a number of open and difficult questions including the following:

- whether the WEU as a sort of a rump organization will continue to exist—for some time at least—with its Treaty remaining in force or whether the WEU will be fully eliminated with some elements of its Treaty included in one way or the other into the EU Treaty?;
- whether all the new institutional elements as proposed in Cologne can be set up without treaty changes? Most of the Member States wish to avoid treaty changes since these would imply referenda to be held on the defence issue alone;
- whether to include the collective defence commitment (Article V) for all Member States? Article V of the modified Brussels Treaty of the WEU might become an article of the EU Treaty, with provision for opt outs, or it could become a protocol attached to the Treaty, signed only by those EU members who are full members of NATO;
- how to resolve the variability of memberships in the EU, WEU and NATO;

- how to structure relations between the EU and NATO;
- the function, location and level of representation (ambassadors, senior officials, deputy political directors) of the new Political/Security Committee in Brussels.

Given the political commitment expressed at Cologne it is likely that solutions to these problems will be found before the end of 2000. There are also other factors making closer defence cooperation likely. There is a continuing squeeze on defence budgets and the recognition that collaboration on procurement is the only way to fund many of the new high-tech weapons systems. A related trend is the establishment of joint operational capabilities, such as the Eurocorps, the Nordic and Baltic battalions, the Anglo–Dutch rapid reaction force and others.

A further important factor in the new moves to establish an ESDI is the attitude of the United States. Long opposed to the concept of ESDI, the US has now become one of its strongest supporters, arguing that in the post-Cold War era, the EU should take on more responsibility for its own security. The US demand for the Europeans to take a larger share of the burden is likely to increase in coming years. The prospects for a genuine ESDI are thus better than ever before. It will take some time, however, before the decisions taken in 1999 will lead to the EU disposing of its own independent military capability.

Certainly there is much to be done to bolster EU effectiveness. EU countries spend $140 per capita a year on defence compared with America's $290, yet the EU possesses only about 10% of the US capacity to deploy and sustain forces overseas. During the Kosovo conflict over 85% of the air power was American. There are also substantial differences between EU Member States spending on defence. (France $708 per head, Spain $196 per head). This has led some observers to argue that the Europeans should increase the percentage of defence spending on research and development and procurement to 40% of defence budgets. And there have also been calls to scrap conscription in favour of professional armed forces.[11]

11. See the Centre for European Reform web site for details of the debate on 'defence convergence criteria'.

7 |

The External Relations of the Union

If one considers the CFSP on its own then any assessment of its early years of operation must inevitably be modest. It has certainly been subjected to some strong criticism, particularly from the US. Jesse Helms, the Chairman of the Senate Foreign Relations Committee, castigated the EU as being 'unable to fight its way out of a paper bag', while Richard Holbrooke, the US chief negotiator in the Bosnian peace process, criticized the EU for its inability to take decisive action in its own backyard and for 'sleeping' during a security crisis between Greece and Turkey.[1] Other Americans have been more complimentary on the EU's expanding role on the world stage, emphasizing its important contribution in terms of 'soft security'.[2] This chapter looks at the external relations of the Union as a whole and provides a positive judgment, arguing that the success of the EU's external policies is reflected in an increasing array of common policies.[3]

It is useful to consider the nature of the EU as an international actor. There is no doubt that along with the US and Japan, the EU is a key player in world trade negotiations. It made a major contribution to the success of the Uruguay Round trade negotiations and is the principal driving force behind proposals to strengthen the World Trade Organization (WTO). It is the prime organizer of the economic rescue of Central and Eastern Europe and the former Soviet Union. It is drawing in its northern, eastern and southern neighbours into a complex web of agreements as a magnet attracts bits of metal. It is the main source of development assistance to the Third World.

1. Helms's remarks were made during the hearings on NATO enlargement in February 1996. Holbrooke was quoted in the *Washington Post* of 23 February 1996.

2. See articles by Ambassadors Eizenstat and Gardner in *the International Herald Tribune* of 2 November 1995 and 30 January 1996 respectively.

3. For a comprehensive review of the EU's external relations see Piening (1997) and Rhodes (1998).

The EU is thus a key player in an increasingly complex international arena covering political, economic, social, environmental and techno-logical issues. As a significant global economic power, it is a much sought after interlocutor on political affairs by an increasing number of countries and regional groupings. However, these developments, imp-ortant in their own right, should not obscure the general failure of the EU to exercise decisive political influence on world events, particularly those involving the use of force.

The EU continues to suffer from what one observer has termed an 'expectations-capability gap'.[4] That is to say, the Union's aggregation of size, economic performance and military arsenals do not automati-cally qualify it as a major world power. Ambitious statements and numerous declarations from Brussels do not compensate for a political system and society in the EU that does not often generate a strong com-mon will, assertiveness and self-confidence in international relations.

Whatever the EU's deficiencies in political coherence, cultural iden-tity and military organization, it certainly does not lack for economic power. It has a larger population (370 million) and GDP than the US. Although only 7% of the world's population, the enlarged EU is the principal provider of foreign direct investment (FDI)—both as a host economy and as a source economy. It provides 53% of all official dev-elopment assistance, holds 37% of global financial reserves, produces 27% of the world's automobiles and is responsible for 19% of world trade (excluding intra-EU trade).[5] The introduction of the euro in January 1999 has led many countries, ranging from China to Cuba, to use it as a reserve currency alongside or in preference to the dollar.

The EU is also extending the scope of its free trade area gradually to the entire continent and even reaching into North Africa. The first step was the creation of the European Economic Area (EEA) to include sev-eral European Free Trade Area (EFTA) countries; the second stage was the extension of the free trade area to Central and Eastern Europe; the third stage envisages exploring the possibility of free trade areas with Russia and Ukraine; and a fourth stage (beginning early in the twenty-first century) would extend this free trade area to the countries of the North African littoral. Taken together this would create a free trade area of just under one billion in population, which would be significantly

4.   The term coined by Christopher Hill (1993).
5.   Figures from Eurostat (1998).

higher than NAFTA in North America or APEC in the Asia-Pacific Region.

External Priorities

The Union has had little choice in defining its external priorities. From the Lisbon European Council in June 1992 to the Vienna European Council in December 1998 there has been a strong emphasis on the EU's immediate neighbourhood. Inevitably the EU had to give first priority to its eastern neighbours who had finally thrown off decades under communist rule. But the EU could not neglect the turmoil in south-east Europe or the instability in the Mediterranean region. It also had to develop a more equal partnership with the US and explore new areas of cooperation with Asia, Africa and Latin America. Moreover the EU found itself playing an increasingly important role in international forums dealing with transnational issues such as the environment, population control, jobs and information technology. There has also been a steady increase in third pillar issues, such as drugs, refugees, asylum seekers and terrorism, which has required the Union to provide a coordinated response with external partners.

Central and Eastern Europe Countries (CEECs)

Since 1989 the European Union has been in the forefront of international efforts to support the reform process and thus to increase stability in the eastern half of the continent. The Union's involvement includes ever closer political links, wide-ranging association or 'Europe' agreements, rapidly growing trade, economic assistance, especially through the PHARE and TACIS programmes,[6] and a pre-accession strategy supported by national partnerships designed to prepare the CEECs for EU membership. The Union also provides considerable financial assistance through the European Investment Bank (EIB) and, collectively, is the largest shareholder in the European Bank for Reconstruction and Development (EBRD). Thus the Union has a range of policies tailored to the situation and needs of each country and which is constantly evolving to meet changing circumstances.

---

6. PHARE and TACIS are the names of the EU's technical assistance programmes to the CEECs and the NIS respectively.

One of the key pillars of the EU's approach towards the CEECs is the Europe Agreements which are in force with 10 countries (Bulgaria, Czech Republic, Estonia, Hungary, Latvia, Lithuania, Poland, Romania, Slovakia and Slovenia). These Europe Agreements are extremely wide-ranging and provide a framework for cooperation in the political, economic, industrial, trade, scientific, technical, environmental and cultural spheres. They also provide a useful preparation for the accession negotiations.

As regards technical assistance, the EU has been spending around one billion euros annually since 1989, concentrating on training, private investment, market access, environment and modernization of agriculture. The European Union is by far the main trading partner of the CEECs, taking over 60% of their exports.

Economically, the accession of Central and East European countries will be a major challenge for them. Together they only add less than 9% of EU GDP and have an average income per head less than 30% of that of the EU. Enlargement will also be a challenge for the Union's own policies, not least its major expenditure policies. In the long term, the enlargement of the internal market to include more than 100 million additional people should bring a new boost and dynamism to the European economy. It will also ensure greater security and stability in Europe (Avery and Cameron 1998).

The EU is also involved in measures to promote regional cooperation in the political, economic and cultural fields. Among the most important of these projects are the Baltic Sea Cooperation Council (BSCC), the Barents Euro-Arctic Council, the Northern Dimension,[7] the Central Free Trade Area (CEFTA) and the Black Sea Economic Cooperation (BSEC) project. These initiatives clearly have a security element in that they deal with concrete risks such as storage of nuclear material and lessen tension by promoting greater transparency and cooperation (Cottey 1999).

Russia/Ukraine/NIS

Developments in Russia, Ukraine and the other Newly Independent States (NIS) also have major implications for the security and prosper-

7.   The Northern Dimension is the name given to the EU's policy towards NW Russia and involves a number of EU Member States in the region, the Baltic States and Poland.

ity of the Union and it remains the EU's intention to establish a strategic political partnership with Russia and Ukraine. These were the first two countries identified for the new CFSP instrument of Common Strategies in 1999.

The EU's interest in the success of the reform process in Russia and Ukraine and the establishment of stable and prosperous systems throughout the NIS is evident.[8] Not only is this an essential element for the security and stability of the European continent and the world as a whole but it also opens up new prospects for more effective international cooperation to address a wide range of global and regional security issues. To this should be added the EU's interest in seeing the emergence of Russia and Ukraine as viable economic partners. At present the economic links between the EU and Russia/Ukraine are rather limited but the potential for a mutually beneficial economic relationship is substantial, once the reform process takes root and the economies of Russia/Ukraine start to recover.

The EU has responded to the situation in Russia, Ukraine and the NIS by negotiating Partnership and Cooperation Agreements (PCA) which provide for cooperation in political, economic and technical issues. The PCA with Russia, for example, is the most ambitious agreement ever signed between the Russian Federation and one of its major world partners. It aims gradually to draw the economies of Russia and the EU closer together by lifting trade barriers, providing a more favourable business environment and promoting the direct investment that the Russian economy so desperately needs. It also paves the way for a potential free trade area, while establishing regular political contacts at all levels and promoting respect for democracy and human rights.

The EU has become the most important trading partner of Russia and the largest provider of technical assistance through the TACIS programme. Priorities have been projects to restructure state enterprises and promote private sector development, agricultural reform, infrastructure (energy, telecommunications, transport), nuclear safety and the environment, public administration reform, social services, education and promotion of democracy.

In addition to the PCA, the Union agreed on a Common Strategy for Russia at the Cologne European Council in June 1999. The added value

---

8. The Newly Independent States (NIS) comprise all former Soviet republics minus the three Baltic states.

of the Common Strategy lay in adopting a cross-pillar approach to Russia supported by contributions from the Member States. The main areas for cooperation were identified as political, especially a strengthened dialogue on foreign and security policy issues, economic reform and global challenges such as the environment and crime. The Ukraine was chosen as the second country to be the subject of a Common Strategy.

The Balkans

As outlined above (Chapter 2) the tragedy of the events in former Yugoslavia dealt a severe blow to the EU's pretensions on the international stage. Yet the EU was the only actor which was involved in all stages of the conflict—from the Delors/Santer mission, the sending of monitors, the peace conference, the imposition of sanctions, to the provision of the largest contingent of UN peacekeepers and IFOR/SFOR/KFOR peace-enforcers—and remains by far the main provider of humanitarian and technical assistance to the region.

The Union will need to give increasing attention to South East Europe for many years, to ensure the success of the Dayton (1995) and Kosovo (1999) agreements and to help stabilize all the countries of the region. The end of hostilities in Bosnia and Kosovo has also opened up the prospect of new trade and cooperation agreements between the EU and the majority of the successor states to former Yugoslavia, as well as Albania. The EU's approach to the region post-Dayton was to emphasize the importance of each country fulfilling the agreements, of taking steps to ensure a functioning democracy with respect for human and minority rights, a market economy and participating in regional cooperation.

The resolution of the Kosovo crisis in June 1999 opened the way for a massive reconstruction effort as well as new policies aimed at supporting regional cooperation and closer ties with the EU. The Union launched a Stability Pact for South East Europe and offered the countries of the region, FYROM in the first instance, a new Stabilization and Association Agreement with the aim of preparing the countries for eventual accession to the EU. The Union also planned to launch a Common Strategy for the Western Balkans (Yugoslavia, Albania, Croatia, FYROM, Bosnia-Herzogovina) in late 1999.

The Mediterranean and Middle East

While concentrating attention in the east, the EU has not neglected its neighbours to the south. The main thrust of EU policy has been to support indigenous economic development (thus creating employment and reducing migratory pressures) coupled with measures to support human rights and the consolidation of democracy in the region.

The Barcelona Euro-Med Conference in November 1995 was an important landmark in the EU's relations with its Mediterranean partners. The outcome of the Conference was agreement on a Declaration and a Work Programme, with the emphasis on three main areas:

- political and security relations: the emphasis was in developing a Security Charter and support for human rights;
- economic and financial relations: the principles of free trade and the market economy, together with substantially increased financial assistance from the EU (4.685 billion Ecus for 1995–99) formed the basis of future relations; the Work Programme outlined areas for increased cooperation (industry, transport, energy, telecommunications, tourism, environment);
- social, cultural and human affairs: the text outlined ways in which civil society would become more involved in the partnership; under this heading sensitive issues such as terrorism, drug trafficking and illegal immigration would be tackled jointly.

The Euro-Med process made a modest start. Despite several ministerial meetings, notably Valletta in 1997 and Palermo in 1998, and numerous official meetings, there was only modest progress to report at the review conference in Stuttgart in April 1999. The Barcelona process complements at multilateral level the development of the EU's bilateral relations with partners. Negotiations for Euro-Mediterranean Association Agreements have been concluded with Israel, Tunisia, Morocco, Jordan and the Palestine Authority. Significant progress has been made with Egypt and Lebanon, while both Algeria and Syria are keen to start negotiations.

Within the broad rubric of the Mediterranean there remain, however, important differences between the various states of the region. Three countries, Turkey, Malta and Cyprus, have applied to join the EU while others, such as Libya, remain pariah states. The EU has thus had to adopt a differentiated approach to states with such wide disparities in terms of size, location, political and economic development.

The Middle East has been one of the most volatile areas in the world in recent years, exemplified by the Iraqi invasion of Kuwait. The Union has a vital interest in securing stability in the region and uninterrupted access to oil supplies. The Gulf War, during which the EU provided substantial humanitarian and economic assistance to the front-line states, has led to increased EU involvement in the region both on the political and economic fronts. The EU is the main trading partner for all countries of the region and is also a key player in the Middle East Peace Process (MEPP). It is the principal provider of assistance, financial and other, to Palestine and organized a successful monitoring mission for the first elections in Palestine. Despite its financial largesse, the EU has been unable to play a decisive role in the MEPP, partly because the US and Israel have not wished the EU, with its more sympathetic attitude towards Palestine, to play such a role.[9]

Transatlantic Relations

With the end of the Cold War relations between the European Union (EU) and the US have changed significantly. The EU's relations with the United States remain the most important of all its external relationships but the previous lopsided security relationship has given way to a more equal and comprehensive partnership. The intensity of the transatlantic partnership is revealed in the number of individual, military and business contacts, educational exchanges, contacts between governments and directly between the EU and the US. Inevitably in such a deep relationship there are also tensions which surface from time to time, such as the 'banana war' of spring 1999. There are a number of commercial areas where the EU and US are natural competitors. There are also some important distinctions between the respective political and social systems, reflecting different traditions and historical experiences. For its part, the US has long regarded itself as the dominant world power and now, with the EU gradually emerging as a more forceful actor on the world stage, particularly following the introduction of the euro, there are some Americans, particularly in the Congress, who find it difficult to adjust to the changed situation. There are also many voices in the US, including several labour unions and right-wing republicans, arguing for a unilateral approach to trade and

9.   For full details of these programmes and policies see the DG1B web site on the Europa Server.

other issues; and increasing American calls for protectionism in the light of the Asian crisis.

In the immediate aftermath of the end of the Cold War, a Transatlantic Declaration was signed in 1990 codifying relations between the Union and the US (a similar Declaration was signed with Canada). The Declaration was not based solely on a common heritage and shared values but also on US recognition of the Union's growing weight in world affairs. Cooperation now takes place in a wide range of areas including foreign and security policy, economics and trade, science and culture to terrorism and drugs. The most visible result of the Declaration which commits both parties 'to inform and consult each other on matters of common political and economic interest' was to initiate a series of half-yearly summit meetings which are now a major feature of the international agenda.

A further strengthening of the EU–US relations took place in Madrid in December 1995 when both sides agreed a New Transatlantic Agenda (NTA) designed to increase transatlantic cooperation in a wide range of areas. The aim of the NTA is to translate common political and economic goals into concrete joint measures that can be reviewed and updated at the regular six-monthly EU–US Summit. The four shared goals which were identified included promoting peace, stability and democracy around the world; responding to global challenges; closer economic relations and contributing to the expansion of world trade; and building people-to-people contacts across the Atlantic (Gardner 1997).[10]

In the NTA the US acknowledged for the first time that the EU and the US are partners in political and security as well as economic matters. The introduction of the euro, the implementation of the Treaty of Amsterdam and the on-going EU enlargement process will further increase the EU's visibility in global affairs and necessitate cooperation with Washington to ensure that EU–US foreign and security policy goals are in line with economic policies. The US has been keen to intensify this cooperation as was demonstrated at the fiftieth anniversary NATO summit in Washington and in the Bonn Declaration of June 1999.

In the area of foreign and security policy, EU–US diplomatic cooperation extends widely even if there are many in the US who are

10. See the Europa server for the full text of the Declaration on the New Transatlantic Agenda.

highly critical of EU efforts in this field and many who wish to preserve the US leadership role. Recent examples of EU–US cooperation include the whole matrix of problems in the Balkans: the reconstruction efforts in Bosnia, the crisis in Kosovo, the instability in Albania. The US and EU mediators (Hill and Petritsch) worked closely together in 1998–99 to bring the conflict parties in Kosovo to the negotiating table. Russia and Ukraine are other areas where there are a number of concrete joint projects under way. Both the EU and US are supporting economic and energy reform in the Ukraine; and working with Russia on nuclear waste in its north-western region. The EU and US also worked closely together in promoting democracy in Slovakia in the late 1990s. The Middle East is another area of cooperation even though there are clear differences in the approach of the EU and US. Other areas of particular interest outside Europe have included Iraq, Iran, developments in Asia (the financial crises, India/Pakistan nuclear testing, human rights in China) and cooperation against terrorism and non-proliferation. In the new areas of soft security the EU and US have intensified their cooperation in the fight against organized crime and drugs.

The Clinton administration has been a strong supporter of closer European integration particularly on the security front. President Clinton backed efforts to establish a European Security and Defence Identity (ESDI) and agreed plans for a Combined Joint Task Force concept at the 1996 Berlin NATO summit which would allow the Europeans to use NATO assets in military operations in which the US did not participate. In the jargon, the ESDI should be 'separable but not separate' from NATO. The US also reacted favourably to Prime Minister Blair's proposals to strengthen the CFSP by developing military capabilities that would allow the EU to act alone.[11] The Washington NATO summit of April 1999 was a clear expression of the US desire to see the EU develop into a genuine partner in order to deal with a growing array of international problems.

EU and US interests are highly developed in the trade field. The EU and the US are the two most important actors in world trade. They are major trade partners for both goods and services and the largest investors in each other's markets. The Transatlantic Partnership on Political Co-operation (TPPC) agreed in Washington in December 1998 contains

---

11. But Madeleine Albright warned in an article in the *Financial Times* of 1 December 1998 that there should be no decoupling, no duplication and no discrimination in establishing a common European defence policy.

a joint EU–US commitment 'to resist the passage of new economic sanction legislation based on foreign policy grounds'. The two sides also agreed on an early warning mechanism at the Cologne EU–US summit in June 1999.

Strengthening EU–US relations is a major challenge for the coming years. It will not be easy because the EU is still developing, and as it develops the US will be called upon to adjust its attitudes. President Clinton, who has spoken of the US desire to have a strong European partner to help resolve European, regional and global security issues, and his successor will need to convince Congress of the importance of a rule-based multilateral trading system. The Europeans will have to develop both the political will and the capabilities to allow the EU to operate a credible and effective CFSP.

Asia, Africa, Latin America

In 1993 Asia became the EU's largest trade partner ahead of the US. In terms of assistance to the region, the EU is the second largest aid donor, behind Japan but far ahead of the US, with most aid concentrated on the poorest countries of the region. In recent years the EU has sought to ensure that its relations with Asia covered political as well as economic, trade and development issues. Political consultations are already held with ASEAN, Japan, China, South Korea, India and Pakistan. The EU also supports the programme in North Korea designed to produce civil nuclear power (KEDO).

The EU's relations with Africa have been developing fast, partly as a result of the Lomé Convention with the African, Caribbean and Pacific (ACP) states, and partly as a result of new challenges such as supporting the transition of South Africa from an apartheid regime to a democratic state. However, there have been some complications as a result of the close ties of individual Member States such as Britain, France, Belgium and Portugal to particular countries, most notably South Africa, Rwanda, East Timor.

The EU is also the principal aid donor to Latin America (60% of all aid in 1998) with the emphasis being on support for rural development and regional cooperation. Recently there has been increased emphasis on support for human rights and the development of democracy. The EU has also negotiated agreements with both Mercosur and the Andean Pact while deepening its relations with Mexico and other central

American countries (dialogue San José). The first EU/Latin America/ Caribbean summit was held in Rio on 29–30 June 1999.

Assessment

As can be seen from this brief review of external relations, the EU has developed strategic approaches to most major regions or countries that cover all three EU pillars. These strategies have normally been developed by the European Commission which has sought to achieve as much coherence as possible in external relations, though there have been times when coherence has been lacking and the Union's approach has been weakened as a result. The Member States have long recognized the importance of speaking with one voice to Russia, Ukraine, Turkey, and so on, even if they sometimes maintain bilateral programmes and contacts. The problems these countries face are ones best tackled by the 15 Member States working together. The EU has also been developing its use of 'conditionality' in external relations to good effect. Inevitably there remain some important differences as regards priorities and interests, which reflect the different histories and traditions of the Member States. Nevertheless, it is clear that taking external relations as a whole the Member States have never been more united in their approach to the outside world. It is thus important to view the CFSP not in isolation but as part of the external relations of the Union.

8 |

Challenges Facing the CFSP

Despite the gradual progress on CFSP, there remain a number of challenges including the definition of the EU's interests: policy priorities; external coherence; representation; democratic control; the implications of enlargement; and timely action to prevent conflicts.

National versus European Interests

In the Treaty of Amsterdam there are mixed references to national versus European interests. Article 13 para. 2 states that the European Council shall decide on Common Strategies to be implemented by the Union in areas where the Member States have important interests in common. The same article also states that if a member of the Council declares that, for important and stated reasons of national policy, it intends to oppose the adoption of a decision to be taken by qualified majority, a vote shall not be taken.

In reality there is rarely a dichotomy between national and European interests. The first attempt to establish the factors which should be taken into account in setting EU priorities was made in a report by Foreign Ministers for the Lisbon European Council in June 1992. The Ministers agreed on the following list: geographical proximity; an important interest in the political and economic stability of a region or country; and the existence of threats to the security interests of the Union. In terms of the first criteria, Ministers agreed a list of priorities including Russia and the former Soviet republics; Central and Eastern Europe; the Balkans; the Maghreb in North Africa and the Middle East. In terms of horizontal interests, the Ministers agreed that priority should be attached to the OSCE, arms control and disarmament, nuclear non-proliferation and control of arms exports.[1]

1.   Appendix 1, Conclusions of the Presidency, Lisbon European Council, 22–23 June 1992. There had been a previous attempt to list priorities at Asolo the previous year.

Nearly all Member States view the Union's CFSP as an opportunity to promote and enhance their national interests within a wider framework. There was swift agreement at the European Council in Vienna in December 1998 on the list of common strategies—Russia, Ukraine, the Western Balkans and the Mediterranean. These priorities, remarkably similar to the 1992 list, include the actual or potential trouble spots in the Union's immediate neighbourhood and reflect the acceptance by the Member States that the Union framework is the most suitable in tackling these problems.

Evidently geography and history play an important role in deciding national priorities. Finland and Sweden are always going to be more concerned about what happens in the Baltic region than the Mediterranean countries. They in turn are always going to be more interested than the Nordic countries in what happens in the Mahgreb. In a Europe without internal frontiers, however, it is increasingly obvious that all Member States have to be interested in what happens in every corner of the Union.

Apart from agreement on promoting stability in the immediate neighbourhood of the Union, there is also a broad EU consensus on the importance of transatlantic relations, of strengthening the rule of law, human rights and of liberal, democratic values outside the EU.

Yet, within the EU there are different attitudes to the CFSP. The smaller Member States are generally the most enthusiastic as they gain an influence through the EU which they would otherwise find difficult to achieve. Germany, Spain and Italy are still very aware of their fascist past and generally prefer to operate in a consensus manner through the Union. The two former world powers, France and the UK, still subscribe to the belief that they should be in a permanent position of leadership, as befits their having a permanent seat on the United Nations Security Council (UNSC) and military capabilities. This sometimes leads to tension between these two states and the others over the direction and purpose of the CFSP.[2] But even they recognize the difficulties of trying to 'go it alone' in dealing with neighbours such as Russia or security issues such as the Western Balkans. Both Paris and London, however, are most unlikely to relinquish their seats on the UNSC in favour of an EU seat. This must remain a distant dream that would only be considered in the event of a more effective and cohesive CFSP.

2.   Germany has also demonstrated a preference for the 'directorate' over EU institutions, e.g. in security matters and in dealing with south-east Europe.

Who Speaks for Europe?

More than a quarter of a century after the oft-quoted remark of Henry Kissinger 'who do I call in Europe?' the question remains unanswered. Depending on which aspect of external policy is on the agenda, third country interlocutors may have to contact the rotating Presidency, Mr CFSP, the Foreign Ministers of Member States, the special EU envoys, the President or one of several other Commissioners dealing with external affairs.

In external trade relations, where the Commission exercises community competence, there is no ambivalence about who speaks for Europe; it is the Commissioner responsible for trade issues who negotiates and speaks for the EU. In the protracted GATT negotiations, which were concluded in 1994, it was Sir Leon Brittan who carried out this role. The US, Japan and other negotiating partners knew that he enjoyed the authority to speak on behalf of all Member States and that he was mandated to conclude an agreement.

In the second pillar, the situation is less clear. Title V of the Amsterdam Treaty states that it is the Presidency who represents the Union in CFSP matters, yet it also allows for a troika of EU Presidency, Commission and Mr CFSP to take on representational tasks. It also entrusts the Council and the Commission to ensure consistency in external policy.

In the early years of CFSP, the Union resorted to a number of different formulae in external representation. The most common formula was the Presidency of the Council. On other occasions, such as the bi-annual summits with the US, Japan or Russia, the Presidency-Commission model was used. There have indeed been meetings with third countries, usually in the margins of the UN, involving all 15 Member States. The troika has been used frequently for fact-finding missions and presenting démarches.

Ad hoc special representatives have also been used with increasing frequency as the missions of Lord Owen, Mr Bildt, Mr Westendorp, Mr Petritsch in former Yugoslavia, and Mr Moratinos in the Middle East, being the most notable examples.[3] The Union enjoys a complicated form of representation in the G7 where four Member States participate

---

3.   Others include Bodo Hombach for south-east Europe and Aldo Ajello for the Great Lakes states in Africa.

in their own right, the Presidency participates when it is not being held by one of these four states, and the Commission is also present.[4]

Finally, there has been unsatisfactory ad hoc representation of the Union in the Contact Group dealing with Bosnia, and another formula, the Quint—UK, France, Germany, Italy, Spain—meeting to discuss relations with Turkey. This trend towards ad hoc groupings could well be accentuated as the EU enlarges and potentially becomes more unwieldy in terms of decision-making. These Contact Group practices have created resentment and apprehension among several Member States fearing they will be used again in other circumstances, and have revived traditional 'big power' attitudes and suspicions.[5] It adds to the perception that diplomacy and defence are dominated by the larger Member States and that national interests are given priority over common action. Of course no one can deny that an important role is played by the larger Member States, two of which are Permanent Members of the United Nations Security Council. On the other hand, the others are opposed to anything resembling a 'directorate' by the larger Member States.

It is not surprising that most third country interlocutors of the Union find its external face baffling. In the Amsterdam conclusions, it was agreed that the Presidency should be assisted by the Secretary General of the Council, who would be given new standing and visibility in foreign policy. The Secretary General would contribute to the formulation, preparation and implementation of decisions, as well as conducting political dialogue with third parties. The Secretary General would also have responsibility for the policy planning and early warning unit. It remains to be seen whether Mr Javier Solana, appointed as Mr CFSP at the Cologne summit in June 1999, will be able to carve out a satisfactory role for himself in terms of EU external representation. It will not be easy to maintain a balance between the role of the Presidency and Mr CFSP (Crowe 1998).[6] As far as Mr Patten is concerned, he made clear during his EP hearings in late August 1999 that he wished to establish the closest possible working relationship with Mr Solana.

---

4.   There is a troika formula for the representation of euroland (the EU states that have adopted the euro as a single currency) in international forums, but there are also voices calling for a single EU representation on financial matters.

5.   Benelux officially complained about the Contact Group structure in 1998.

6.   Mr Solana was also nominated Secretary General of the WEU in late 1999, a move which was designed to facilitate the integration of the WEU into the EU.

The Presidency

With 15 Member States of differing sizes, global experience and administrative capacities, it is not surprising that there are substantial differences in each member's operation of the Presidency. All tend to present their efforts as more a reflection of national than EU achievements. The six-month period in office is rarely sufficient to make a profound impact (or do much harm) to EU business. A running-in period is needed before the Presidency becomes fully effective and, by that time, the Presidency's term of office is already well advanced. The domestic electoral cycle also plays a role. In 1997 the new Labour government had to take over the Presidency reins within a few weeks of taking office. The new German government composed of Social Democrats and Greens, who had never been in government before, were also propelled into the Presidency in 1999 with little or no previous experience.

There is often little correlation between the size of a country and its performance during the Presidency. Indeed one could argue that the more successful Presidencies in recent years were those run by the smaller and medium-sized Member States. In the mid-1990s, both Germany and France suffered from the burden of holding national elections during their term of office. However, there is a problem of credibility in the eyes of some third country partners when the Presidency is held by a small Member State. An example was the reluctance of the US to schedule a routine EU–US summit in December 1997 partly because the Presidency was held by Luxembourg and the Commission would also be represented by its Luxembourg President, Jacques Santer. Some micro-states such as Malta might face similar problems in future.

Despite the comments above concerning size, the capacity of the diplomatic service holding the Presidency does have an impact on the ability of the Union to operate an effective CFSP. As the Union's tentacles stretch into every corner of the globe, those Member States with global diplomatic capabilities clearly enjoy an advantage. Luxembourg, for example, has to rely mainly on the Dutch missions abroad for diplomatic reporting. Smaller Member States are also likely to rely more on the support of the Council Secretariat which, although it has expanded since 1993, has only modest capacities.

Policy Planning

One of the problems in the CFSP is that there is little pooled information, apart from that which is circulated on the Coreu network. This means that ministers and officials come to meetings with briefing papers of widely varying quality, and which are written from a national perspective. Inevitably it is the larger Member States with the necessary resources which make the greatest contribution in terms of information provided. The establishment of a policy planning capacity in the Treaty of Amsterdam was designed partly to rectify these problems.

The background to the establishment of the Policy Planning and Early Warning Unit (PPEWU) was the widely held view that the Union had problems setting clear foreign policy priorities and failed to anticipate and react in a timely manner to various crises, notably Yugoslavia. The idea for a PPEWU found widespread support in the Reflection Group and IGC. The arguments in favour of establishing such a unit included: that it would help to provide a common European assessment and analysis of foreign and security policy; it would provide the Presidency and General Affairs Council (GAC) with option papers; and it would provide an early warning function.

The provisions of the PPEWU are set out in Appendix 3. It will take some time to resolve the problem areas which were not covered in the Amsterdam declaration. These include: the access of the PPEWU to comprehensive, relevant and timely information; the lack of a budget; how to overcome differences of view whether between its 20-strong staff—drawn from Member States, the Commission, Council Secretariat and WEU—or between the PPEWU and its head, the High Representative (Mr CFSP); and how to achieve a genuine role in the confused policy-making process of the Union. It will be important to maintain close cooperation with the Commission planners and those from Member States.

Clearly much will depend on how Mr Solana develops his role and on the quality of the unit's output. There are many tasks which the unit could undertake including analysing developments in areas of interest to the CFSP, signalling early warnings of trouble spots, assessing priorities, preparing policy option papers and maintaining links to the academic and research community.[7]

7.   See the report by Cottey (1998), Lodge and Flynn (1998) and the report by Dolan (1997).

The Problems of Coherence and Consistency

The pillar structure of the EU, the shared competences between the Union and Member States, the different policy-making and decision-making structures aggravate the problems of coherence and consistency in external relations. Although the CFSP contains provisions for taking joint actions and common positions, these are not instruments as such. Most instruments are in the hands of the Commission, which also controls most expenditure on external relations. It is perhaps worth considering the range of instruments available to the Union.

On the diplomatic front the EU has so far used the following: declarations and statements; démarches; troika missions; special envoys; diplomatic recognition/sanctions; political dialogue; sponsoring peace conferences; mediating in disputes; sending election observers; sending cease-fire monitors. On the economic side the EU has also developed an impressive array of instruments, including trade and cooperation agreements; association or Europe agreements; tariff reductions/quota increases; granting of a generalized system of preference (GSP); provision of aid, loans, technical assistance. These may be matched on the negative side by embargoes, sanctions, boycotts, delaying or suspending agreements, increasing tariffs and lowering quotas, withdrawing GSP, reducing aid, loans and technical assistance.

Conditionality of aid and trade instruments has become more and more important in recent years as the EU, under pressure from the European Parliament, has sought to influence the behaviour of third world countries particularly with regard to democratic development, human and minority rights.

The problems of coherence and consistency were supposed to have been addressed by the Amsterdam Treaty but it remains to be seen whether the General Affairs Council will be able to fulfil its treaty obligations and cooperate effectively with the Commission to this end (Krenzler and Schneider 1994).

The Role of the European Parliament

One of the continuing deficits in CFSP is the lack of transparency and democratic oversight. The Maastricht Treaty allowed the European Parliament (EP) only a very limited role in the CFSP but there are signs that the Parliament will exploit its opportunities to the full in order to assert itself. At present, the EP can make its voice heard through its reports and resolutions, through its parliamentary contacts with third countries and through its participation in the EU's budgetary process. The EP often invites important visitors to speak on foreign policy and sends delegations to observe elections or on fact-finding missions. By skilful use of its budgetary powers the EP has also been able to exert some influence on the means to implement the CFSP. The EP has sought to establish a working relationship with the High Representative, with the EU's special envoys, and with Heads of Commission delegations (Gourlay 1999).

It would be a useful step forward if there were an annual report and debate on the CFSP in the European Parliament and simultaneously in the parliaments of Member States. This could be done on the basis of a report on CFSP priorities and performance drawn up by the PPEWU. It would have the advantage of engaging foreign ministers more closely in the CFSP, explaining it to a wider domestic audience and thus securing increased support from the citizens of the EU. Opinion polls regularly reveal high public support for a stronger EU voice in international affairs.[8] It would also be useful to establish a forum for Non-Governmental Organizations (NGOs) to express their views on a regular basis. Both moves would help raise the consciousness of the CFSP in the minds of the public and provide increased legitimacy for Union actions.

The Implications of Enlargement

An enlarged EU with 25-plus Member States will have important implications for the CFSP. Overall, enlargement should lead to greater security in Europe as a result of increasing political stability and economic prosperity. Enlargement should increase the weight and influence of the EU in international affairs, bring the Union into more direct contact with neighbours, with whom the EU will have new or extended borders, including Russia, Ukraine and Turkey, and reshape the geopolitical map of Europe. An enlarged Union will have direct frontiers with Russia, Ukraine, Belarus, and enjoy direct access to the Black Sea that will lead to intensified contacts with the countries of the Caucasus and Central Asia. An enlarged EU will also surround the Kaliningrad

---

8.   See the results of the Eurobarometer polls published by the Information Directorate General (DGX) of the European Commission.

oblast, which is part of Russia, and will contain several hundred thousand Russians, living mainly in Estonia and Latvia.

In addition, an enlarged EU, with a significantly higher population than the US or Japan, will further increase its status as the largest trading group in the world. The increased weight and influence in external relations that should accrue to an enlarged EU will be dependent, however, on the Union developing a more coherent approach to its external relations, mobilizing all the instruments at its disposal, and ensuring the efficient functioning of the new arrangements agreed in Amsterdam for the CFSP. Regrettably the IGC did not specifically address the implications of enlargement.

One of the major problems facing the CFSP is how to operate policy in this sensitive area in an enlarged Union with perhaps 25 or more Member States. The problems include: defining the common interests in a much more heterogeneous Union stretching from Portugal to Estonia, and Sweden to Cyprus; rapid CFSP decision-making with so many Member States operating on intergovernmental lines; and microstates holding the rotating Presidency.

Of the new candidate countries, only two, Cyprus and Malta, have neutrality provisions in their constitution. With the previous enlargement, on the accession of Austria, Sweden and Finland, this was resolved in the enlargement negotiations by a compromise between those who wished to see the neutral applicants enter into 'specific and binding commitments with regard to the candidates political commitment and legal capacity to fulfil the obligations of the CFSP' and those who were prepared to accept the assurances of the applicants at face value (Cameron 1995).

The Commission opinions on Austria, Sweden and Finland were all favourable. The CFSP chapters drew attention to their general orientation towards the EU, their active membership of the UN and other international organizations and their record in contributing to the developing world. The dialogue between the Union and the applicants revealed a wide consensus on foreign and security policy issues and there was general agreement that the EFTA applicants would strengthen the CFSP. All had accomplished diplomatic services and would be able to act as President without any serious problems. All were active members in the international arena—UN, OSCE, OECD, and so on— with considerable experience of peacekeeping, development aid and specialized knowledge and experience of key areas to the east and south-east of the Community. Given the increasing emphasis on financial and economic diplomacy, the applicants were expected to provide increased resources to strengthen the CFSP.

But there were some concerns about their policy of neutrality and the possible implications for the Union's attempts to forge a common defence policy. In November 1993 the Belgian Presidency conducted talks with the three countries, which led to the following formula:

> The Union and Austria, Sweden, Finland and Norway agree that:
> accession to the Union should strengthen the internal coherence of the Union and its capacity to act effectively in foreign and security policy
> - the acceding states will from the time of their accession be ready and able to participate fully and actively in the CFSP as defined in the TEU
> - the acceding states will, on accession, take on in their entireity and without reservation the objectives of the Treaty, the provisions of its Title V, and the relevant declarations attached to it
> - the acceding states will be ready and able to support the specific policies of the Union in force at the time of their accession
>
> With regard to member states' obligations deriving from the TEU concerning the implementation of the CFSP it is understood that on the day of accession the legal framework of the acceding countries will be compatible with the acquis.[9]

This latter clause related to concerns about whether the new countries would be able to apply the sanctions policy of the Union. Although the three new countries have not modified their basic stance on neutrality since joining the Union, there has been a steady trend, notably among elite opinion, in favour of a more cooperative attitude towards European security institutions. All three countries joined the Partnership for Peace (PfP) and Sweden and Finland were the originators of the proposal that the EU should take over responsibility for the Petersberg Tasks. It is likely that the new candidates would be required to sign up to a similar declaration as outlined above.

With the publication of *Agenda 2000* in July 1997 the Commission set out its views on the EU's priorities for the coming decade and recommended, on the basis of individual Opinions on the candidate countries, that accession negotiations should commence early in 1998 with Poland, Hungary, Estonia, the Czech Republic and Slovenia plus

---

9.   Joint declaration on the CFSP annexed to the Accession Treaties, Corfu 24 June 1994, *OJ* C 241 29.8.1994.

Cyprus which already received a positive opinion in 1993. The remaining five candidates, Latvia, Lithuania, Slovakia, Romania and Bulgaria would be subjected to an annual review and could join those already at the negotiating table when sufficient progress had been made. These recommendations were endorsed by the European Council in Luxembourg in December 1997.[10]

In the CFSP chapters of the Commission's Opinions, all candidates received a positive assessment as they had been closely following the CFSP for some time and had used the opportunities to associate themselves with EU decisions and declarations to demonstrate their general and specific support for the CFSP. Given the predominantly declaratory nature of the CFSP, this was not a difficult hurdle for them to overcome.

With some CEECs having regained their national independence only a few years ago, their sensitivity regarding national sovereignty is rather different compared to 'older' European states. This is due partly to different historical experiences and the public perception of sovereignty. Even during the period of Soviet domination, the CEECs enjoyed different levels of freedom including political and economic reforms. Moreover, in more than one case, political independence resulted in the rebirth of nation states. Czech independence dates back to 1918, Estonia has a record of only some 28 years of national independence, while Slovenia has never been an independent state. Thus in many countries nation-building (and state building) has to be carried out simultaneously with integration into EU and global structures. Sharing sovereignty in foreign and security policy could well pose domestic problems but this could also be eased with integration into European institutions.

Given the strategic importance and potential new security risks emanating from the region, it is important that the enlarged Union does not neglect its relations with the Mediterranean and pursues the policies agreed at Barcelona with vigour. The proposed Common Strategy for the Mediterranean is designed to focus greater attention on the region. The Union is also likely to become more involved in the Middle East, notably as an important actor in the peace process, not least because of its trade agreements, technical and financial assistance. While the future of the Balkans is difficult to predict, EU enlargement will certainly increase rather than diminish the importance of the region to the Union.

10. For a review of the enlargement process see Avery and Cameron (1998).

The enlargement process, combined with EU support for regional cooperation (Stability Pact), should contribute to greater overall security and stability.

Enlargement is already encouraging new thinking on the question of what is precisely meant by 'security' in the post-Cold War era. Since the dangers of ethnic conflict, civil unrest, economic collapse and environmental disaster are still greater in the eastern part of Europe than in the West, it seems likely that these concerns will be accorded a higher priority on the European security agenda than hitherto. Because their borders will form part of the Union's external frontier after accession, candidate countries are already being urged by the Union, as part of the accession process, to enforce measures against organized crime, drug trafficking and illegal immigration.

The European Conference, established by the Luxembourg European Council in December 1997, is a forum where Member States and candidate countries can discuss cross-border issues, including CFSP, environmental issues, crime, drugs and regional cooperation. One of the aims behind its creation was to include Turkey in a dialogue on such issues but Ankara, angered at the EU not having granted Turkey 'candidate status', refused to participate. In relation to the CFSP, the Conference, which met for the first time in March 1998, facilitates closer involvement of candidate countries on declarations and actions.

According to *Agenda 2000*, the candidate countries are required to make every effort to resolve border disputes or submit to compulsory jurisdiction. The Commission's November 1998 report on candidate countries' progress towards accession noted that several disputes of this kind had yet to be resolved, including the dispute between Slovenia and Croatia over Piran Bay; between Latvia and Lithuania over maritime borders; and between Hungary and Slovakia over the Gabcikovo dam.

For CEECs, 'enlargement' in the field of hard security is likely to focus primarily on NATO enlargement rather than on the EU. However, there could well be a difference in enthusiasm for participation in EU defence structures between those candidate countries (Poland, Hungary, Czech Republic) which have joined NATO and those which have not. Much will depend on the credibility of the new proposals for a common European security and defence policy endorsed by the Cologne European Council in June 1999.

Conflict Prevention

In recent years, largely as a result of events in the Balkans, the EU has paid more and more attention to conflict prevention even though the development of effective early warning systems and the utility of early warning are problematic (Cottey 1998). Early warning is of little value unless it is linked to policy formulation and results in timely and effective action. Many conflicts have been widely predicted and the failure to prevent them has lain not so much in the lack of early warning but rather in the absence of political will to take effective action—Kosovo being only the most recent and obvious example. The early warning of conflicts is also a complex issue, requiring analysis of the interaction of a wide range of political, economic, military, environmental and social factors. Thus, there is a need to assess a range of conflict indicators and to analyse their interaction and overall impact. Numerous actors may be involved in and contribute to the provision of early warning (national foreign ministries, international organisations, think tanks and academics, and so on) and there is a need for better cooperation between these actors. Finally, even if decision-makers agree on the need for action in response to warnings, determining the appropriate policy response often remains difficult.

Another problem of conflict prevention is deciding when to take action. Too often preventative diplomacy tends to focus on situations where violent conflict is already likely or imminent and on strategies designed to address the immediate threat of violence. While such strategies may make a vital contribution to preventing the outbreak of violence in the short term, they are unlikely, in themselves, to address the underlying causes of conflict.

In recent years, there has been a growing recognition that effective conflict prevention requires a more comprehensive approach addressing the underlying causes of instability and conflict, not simply the more immediate causes or symptoms of violence. Policies for long-term structural prevention may include promoting democracy, good governance and human rights; encouraging policy reform concerning internal security forces, judicial systems and armed forces; promoting economic development and provision of people's basic needs (health, welfare, housing and so on); and encouraging environmental protection and environmentally sustainable economic policies. The political-economic nature of many of these issues highlights the importance of development policies as instruments for conflict prevention and the need to integrate development policies into wider conflict prevention strategies.

Since the early 1990s, the EU has used the wide-ranging instruments at its disposal to play an increasingly important role in developing long-term, structural approaches to conflict prevention. This has resulted in a number of new initiatives, which have conflict prevention as one of their core concerns. They include the Stability Pact (see above), the PHARE and TACIS assistance programmes, particularly those supporting democratic institutions, the Euro-Mediterranean Partnership programme and the Council declaration on Conflict Prevention in Africa. There have also been a number of initiatives to promote (sub)regional cooperation on the Union's periphery—the Barents, Baltic and Black Sea schemes—and support for regional cooperation in Africa—the Organization of African Unity (OAU), the East African Community (EAC) and the Southern African Development Community (SADC). There are increasing efforts also to integrate conflict prevention into EU development instruments and policies. Promoting peace and stability is a central objective in the Commission's mandate for the renegotiation of the Lomé Convention in 1999–2000.

Based on an earlier proposal from the European Parliament, the European Commission has also supported (since January 1997) a new initiative—the Conflict Prevention Network (CPN). The CPN (which since January 1998 has been expanded into an EU Analysis and Evaluation Centre of which the CPN remains one part) seeks to promote conflict prevention by bringing together policy-makers within the Commission and academic and non-governmental experts to discuss preventative policy options.[11]

Assessment

Since its inception, the CFSP has been in an almost permanent state of flux. It has made steady if unspectacular progress despite the Member States having mixed views on its scope and operation. It has begun to define common external interests, to act in a more coherent manner and to allow the EP a slightly greater say in CFSP. The arrival of Javier Solana as Mr CFSP should give the EU a strengthened capacity for

11. See the annual reports on CPN published by the Stiftung Wissenschaft und Politik, Ebenhausen, Germany; also the annual CFSP reports published by the European Parliament.

creative diplomacy. The GAC will have to reflect on how to best support Mr CFSP in his role. Enlargement will be a major challenge to the CFSP involving the deepening of relations with countries such as Russia and Ukraine, as well as highlighting the need for structural changes. There is a real danger than an enlarged Union would be paralysed in CFSP decision-making unless there were further reforms. As regards conflict prevention, the Member States need to translate their lofty rhetoric into concrete and timely action. They might well ask themselves whether they should not have given more priority to south east Europe in the 1990s, and whether the present structures are adequate for crisis management. This refers not only to the civilian aspects but the military and police aspects of crisis management. With nearly two million men and women in uniform the 15 Member States of the Union struggled to provide 2.5% of that number as an intervention force in Kosovo.

9 |

The Future of the CFSP

The idea of a credible and effective CFSP has been a constant theme of European integration since the early 1950s. After the failure to create political and defence communities in 1954 the EU developed its external relations slowly, with the emphasis on trade and development policies. From the 1970s onwards the Member States began to recognize the importance of closer cooperation in the more traditional domains of foreign policy. The modest experience of the EPC laid the framework for the establishment of the CFSP at Maastricht. But even before the ink was dry on the Treaty, there were calls for changes to make the CFSP more effective and to allow the EU 'to assert its identity on the international stage'. The changes agreed at Amsterdam should enable the Union to enter the new millennium with a more effective CFSP, provided that the Member States develop the necessary political will and the problems of coherence and consistency are resolved.

The debate about the CFSP, however, reflects unresolved questions about the EU's development. Is the high tide of integration past, as many Eurosceptics hope? Or is the functionalist trend so strong that the Union will have to develop even more spheres of competence? As regards foreign policy, is the Union likely to remain essentially a civil power, with an external role largely confined to the economic sphere? Or do the Member States wish to transform the EU into a major global power? Should the Union have the long-term aim of creating its own diplomatic service and armed forces, as the European Parliament and Commission President Prodi have proposed? Or should it limit its ambitions to cooperating on a range of areas of mutual interest?

There remain considerable differences of view between the Member States on these questions. While the UK and France, with their global and colonial traditions, added to their nuclear status and membership of the UNSC, would prefer the EU to enjoy a global reach (at least on some issues), Member States with no such traditions or status would be content with the EU playing a regional role, with the emphasis on the exercise of civil as opposed to military power. At the same time the small and medium-sized states obtain proportionally greater influence by operating through the CFSP. This will also be true for the vast majority of applicant countries.

However, it is very clear from the case of former Yugoslavia that if an international actor cannot back up its diplomacy with military force, it will suffer from a lack of credibility and influence. The prospect of the Union trying to emulate the US in power projection is unrealistic as aside from any other questions, it would involve a significant increase in military expenditure which Member States are unwilling to accept. Moreover, despite the growing convergence of interests, each member state retains primary responsibility for the conduct of foreign affairs and for its own defence; and each state has its own distinctive network of external relations, based on history, geography and its own view of its national interests. Also, the EU does not yet have a common defence industry or an effective common procurement policy.

Although the European Council has stated its intent that there should be a major strengthening and extension of the Union's external role, the arguments over CFSP issues which were demonstrated at Maastricht and Amsterdam suggest that this will not be an easy task. The continuing ability of Member States to behave independently on the world stage, combined with the extent of disagreements on CFSP issues (embracing sharp disagreements on institutional and procedural issues as well as on substantive questions of policy) has often been revealed in recent years.

Nevertheless there are a number of trends working in favour of a more integrated approach including the convergence of views among the most important Member States (St Malo being a good example), the added strength from speaking with one voice in a shrinking world, the strong public support for a common European security and defence policy, the ever-increasing cost of new weaponry which is forcing governments to cooperate more and more in the procurement field and the revised position of the United States.

The trend towards greater integration is also being pushed by the changed nature of the foreign policy agenda. In contrast to the Cold War era, ministerial meetings today are dominated by requests for association agreements, economic and technical assistance, balance-of-payments support, the safety of nuclear reactors, and similar topics. This agenda can clearly be fulfilled best by a community approach as opposed to 15 different national policies. By acting together, for example on Russia, the EU is capable of producing the necessary resources to influence outcomes in a variety of situations. This can vary from large-scale macroeconomic assistance to discreet diplomatic démarches about human rights abuses.

It is also encouraging that even the larger Member States recognize the benefits of acting together. In his inaugural speech to the European Parliament in January 1999, the German Foreign Minister, Joschka Fischer, called for a strengthened CFSP stating that

> only a Union that is capable of taking action in the foreign policy sphere can safeguard peace in Europe and bring its growing weight to bear on the world stage. Even the large Member States of the EU will be increasingly incapable of representing their interests and preserving peace in an increasingly global world. In the multipolar world of the twenty-first century the EU must therefore become an independent entity capable of political action. We must prepare ourselves for this by establishing a CFSP worthy of the name.[1]

If one takes Fisher's vision seriously, then ultimately the CFSP may lead to a European diplomatic service with common EU missions in third countries and international organizations. A nascent European diplomatic service is already in place with different strands. There is Mr CFSP and the Council Secretariat, notably the PPEWU; there is the Commission with its large network of delegations; and there are of course the impressive resources of the Member States. To ease the burden on the Presidency, one could envisage EU task forces being established drawing on the resources of the Member States, Commission and Council.

The nature of diplomacy is changing fast. Within the EU, diplomatic missions have changed their role fundamentally and now contain representatives of many 'domestic' ministries who also maintain direct links with Brussels. Leaders meet and talk together far more frequently than before thus reducing the scope for ambassadors to play a meaningful role. There is also the cost factor. As diplomatic services are being squeezed, it makes good sense to share facilities and resources.

There are many who question the wisdom of the present 15, or in future 25, Member States each maintaining their own embassies in up

1.   *Agence Europe*, 19 January 1999.

to 184 countries when they are supposed to be operating a CFSP. A golden opportunity was missed in the early 1990s with the collapse of the Soviet Union and the creation of 15 newly independent states. Some Member States were prepared to consider joint embassies in some of these new states but no consensus was reached. So far there have been only a few examples of cooperation, for example in Abuja in Nigeria, where several Member States share a common embassy complex. This is clearly an area for closer cooperation in future. A related matter is the sharing of premises, and medical, education and transport facilities. A further step would be joint reporting. It does not make sense for each Member State to maintain several diplomatic officers undertaking political and economic reporting in third countries whose reports are sent back to desk officers in capitals who then take the reports to the monthly CFSP working groups in Brussels.

There is also considerable scope for increased cooperation, as stated in the Treaty, between the Commission's delegations and the missions of Member States. There are, for example, ideas afoot for the Commission delegations to offer to host diplomats from Member States who do not have their own missions. The growing importance of third pillar activities will also impact on external representation. A Europe without internal borders necessitates a common approach towards visas, immigration and asylum seekers. There are already discussions about creating a common Consular Service and the idea of a common External Frontier Service has also been suggested.[2]

The prospects for a further strengthening of the CFSP are good. It remains to be seen, however, if the agreements at the Cologne European Council on security and defence will be translated into action and whether a beefed up CFSP will lead to significant changes in the substance, direction or style of the Union's external policy. Whatever the outcome of the debate, there remains a broad consensus in favour of a strengthened CFSP. There is also a consensus that the Union has an increasing number of shared interests, that the Union has something distinctive to contribute to the resolution of major international disputes and to the construction of the post-Cold War European security architecture.

The dilemma is the conflict between the Cold War and post-Cold War paradigms. Arguably the CFSP should be shaped to match new

2. See the annual reports on CFSP by the European Parliament for the development of these ideas.

models of security, embracing consideration of various external and internal threats to the well-being of European populations, such as cross-border crime, terrorism and ethnic conflict. The development of the Union's CFSP must be based on recognition that, at least for the foreseeable future, the US is likely to remain the key external actor in most major international crises (not least because it is regarded as such by most other international actors).

In many if not most cases the EU and US will achieve more by working with rather than against each other. This does not mean blind acceptance of, or support for US policies. It means a creative dialogue and engagement, in which European policy positions can be vigorously asserted and European expertise and resources deployed within the context of this post-Cold War transatlantic partnership.

Given these differences, one approach might be for the Union to limit the CFSP for the time being to a small number of agreed priorities which would be tackled in common. Another idea would be for the EU to focus more on conflict prevention, pointing to a number of successful EU initiatives in this field, such as its policy of political conditionality, the Stability Pact, the administration of Mostar and its support for regional cooperation ventures.

It is important to remember that the EU was not conceived as a mechanism for European power projection. Its main aim was the prevention of war through peaceful reconciliation based on economic recovery and progress through gradual integration. For this reason the EC was often viewed in a more favourable light than the two superpowers during the Cold War. If anything, the ending of the Cold War has increased the EU's attractiveness as an international actor. Its relative weakness as a military power has seemed less important than its economic development.

Given the changing nature of security in the post-Cold War era, the EU is clearly well placed to deal with the new panoply of security risks. For 40 years security was largely seen in purely military terms—balance of power, deterrence—but with the collapse of communism a range of new security risks have emerged which require a multi-faceted approach in response, encompassing not only military but also political, economic, social and environmental means. The EU, which is the very negation of the old balance of power approach to international relations, is well placed to take the lead in cooperation with other institutions dealing with European security.

The new European security system will need an anchor of stability which, as far as the European continent is concerned, can only be provided by the European Union. To be able to fulfil this role, the European Union will have to develop and to act in close partnership not only with the US, but also with countries such as Russia, the Ukraine and Turkey thus providing the foreign policy of the European Union with a vital transatlantic and all-European dimension, complemented by a strong Mediterranean component.

In the 1970s and 1980s West Germany used to be described as 'an economic giant but a political dwarf'. The same description could have been applied to the Union in the 1980s. Just as the unification of Germany has given the Germans a stronger political voice, so too should the political weight of the Union increase in parallel with its moves to both enlargement and deeper integration. This will require a genuine commitment by the Member States to ensure an effective CFSP if the Union is to pursue an active, rather than reactive, role on the international stage. As the main provider of 'soft' security, the EU is already performing an important stabilizing function but it will also have to develop a 'hard' security component if it is to act credibly on the world stage.

The CFSP has been in operation for a relatively short period of time, less than a decade. It should be regarded as a process, one that will take time to meet the lofty ideals in the Treaty. But the initial years demonstrate that the CFSP is heading in the right direction. It would be wrong, however, to view the CFSP in isolation from the external relations of the Union as a whole. Over the range of its external affairs the Union has never been more united in its history than it is today. A Union with 350 million citizens, the largest trading bloc in the world and now with a single currency, the largest provider of development aid and humanitarian assistance, cannot escape from playing a greater role in foreign and security policy. The Cologne European Council demonstrated the political commitment to achieve results. History will judge Europe's leaders harshly if they fail to deliver.

Appendix 1

Title V of the Treaty of Amsterdam

Provisions on a common foreign and security policy

Article 11

1. The Union shall define and implement a common foreign and security policy covering all areas of foreign and security policy, the objectives of which shall be:

   - to safeguard the common values, fundamental interests, independence and integrity of the Union in conformity with the principles of the United Nations Charter;
   - to strengthen the security of the Union in all ways;
   - to preserve peace and strengthen international security, in accordance with the principles of the United Nations Charter, as well as the principles of the Helsinki Final Act and the objectives of the Paris Charter, including those on external borders;
   - to promote international cooperation;
   - to develop and consolidate democracy and the rule of law, and respect for human rights and fundamental freedoms.

2. The Member States shall support the Union's external and security policy actively and unreservedly in a spirit of loyalty and mutual solidarity.

   The Member States shall work together to enhance and develop their mutual political solidarity. They shall refrain from any action which is contrary to the interests of the Union or likely to impair its effectiveness as a cohesive force in international relations.

   The Council shall ensure that these principles are complied with.

Article 12

The Union shall pursue the objectives set out in Article 11 by:

   - defining the principles of and general guidelines for the common foreign and security policy;
   - deciding on common strategies;

-   adopting joint actions;
-   adopting common positions;
-   strengthening systematic cooperation between Member States in the conduct of policy.

Article 13

(1)   The European Council shall define the principles of and general guidelines for the common foreign and security policy, including for matters with defence implications.

(2)   The European Council shall decide on common strategies to be implemented by the Union in areas where the Member States have important interests in common.

Common strategies shall set out their objectives, duration and the means to be made available by the Union and the Member States.

(3)   The Council shall take the decisions necessary for defining and implementing the common foreign and security policy on the basis of the general guidelines defined by the European Council.

The Council shall recommend common strategies to the European Council and shall implement them, in particular by adopting joint actions and common positions.

The Council shall ensure the unity, consistency and effectiveness of action by the Union.

Article 14

(1)   The Council shall adopt joint actions. Joint actions shall address specific situations where operational action by the Union is deemed to be required. They shall lay down their objectives, scope, the means to be made available to the Union, if necessary their duration, and the conditions for their implementation.

(2)   If there is a change in circumstances having a substantial effect on a question subject to joint action, the Council shall review the principles and objectives of that action and take the necessary decisions. As long as the Council has not acted, the joint action shall stand.

(3)   Joint actions shall commit the Member States in the positions they adopt and in the conduct of their activity.

(4)   The Council may request the Commission to submit to it any appropriate proposals relating to the common foreign and security policy to ensure the implementation of a joint action.

(5)   Whenever there is any plan to adopt a national position or take national action pursuant to a joint action, information shall be provided in time to allow, if

necessary, for prior consultations within the Council. The obligation to provide prior information shall not apply to measures which are merely a national transposition of Council decisions.

(6) In cases of imperative need arising from changes in the situation and failing a Council decision, Member States may take the necessary measures as a matter of urgency having regard to the general objectives of the joint action. The Member State concerned shall inform the Council immediately of any such measures.

(7) Should there be any major difficulties in implementing a joint action, a Member State shall refer them to the Council which shall discuss them and seek appropriate solutions. Such solutions shall not run counter to the objectives of the joint action or impair its effectiveness.

Article 15
The Council shall adopt common positions. Common positions shall define the approach of the Union to a particular matter of a geographical or thematic nature. Member States shall ensure that their national policies conform to the common positions.

Article 16
Member States shall inform and consult one another within the Council on any matter of foreign and security policy of general interest in order to ensure that the Union's influence is exerted as effectively as possible by means of concerted and convergent action.

Article 17
(1) The common foreign and security policy shall include all questions relating to the security of the Union, including the progressive framing of a common defence policy, in accordance with the second subparagraph, which might lead to a common defence, should the European Council so decide. It shall in that case recommend to the Member States the adoption of such a decision in accordance with their respective constitutional requirements.

The Western European Union (WEU) is an integral part of the development of the Union providing the Union with access to an operational capability notably in the context of paragraph 2. It supports the Union in framing the defence aspects of the common foreign and security policy as set out in this Article. The Union shall accordingly foster closer institutional relations with the WEU with a view to the possibility of the integration of the WEU into the Union, should the European Council so decide. It shall in that case recommend to the Member States the adoption of such a decision in accordance with their respective constitutional requirements.

The policy of the Union in accordance with this Article shall not prejudice the specific character of the security and defence policy of certain Member States and shall respect the obligations of certain Member States, which see their common defence realised in the North Atlantic Treaty Organisation (NATO), under the North Atlantic Treaty and be compatible with the common security and defence policy established within that framework.

The progressive framing of a common defence policy will be supported, as Member States consider appropriate, by cooperation between them in the field of armaments.

(2)   Questions referred to in this Article shall include humanitarian and rescue tasks, peacekeeping tasks and tasks of combat forces in crisis management, including peacemaking.

(3)   The Union will avail itself of the WEU to elaborate and implement decisions and actions of the Union which have defence implications.

The competence of the European Council to establish guidelines in accordance with Article 13 shall also obtain in respect of the WEU for those matters for which the Union avails itself of the WEU.

When the Union avails itself of the WEU to elaborate and implement decisions of the Union on the tasks referred to in paragraph 2 all Member States of the Union shall be entitled to participate fully in the tasks in question. The Council, in agreement with the institutions of the WEU, shall adopt the necessary practical arrangements to allow all Member States contributing to the tasks in question to participate fully and on an equal footing in planning and decision-taking in the WEU.

Decisions having defence implications dealt with under this paragraph shall be taken without prejudice to the policies and obligations referred to in paragraph 1, third subparagraph.

(4)   The provisions of this Article shall not prevent the development of closer cooperation between two or more Member States on a bilateral level, in the framework of the WEU and the Atlantic Alliance, provided such cooperation does not run counter to or impede that provided for in this Title.

(5)   With a view to furthering the objectives of this Article, the provisions of this Article will be reviewed in accordance with Article 48.

Article 18

(1)   The Presidency shall represent the Union in matters coming within the common foreign and security policy.

(2)   The Presidency shall be responsible for the implementation of decisions taken under this Title; in that capacity it shall in principle express the position of the Union in international organisations and international conferences.

(3) The Presidency shall be assisted by the Secretary-General of the Council who shall exercise the function of High Representative for the common foreign and security policy.

(4) The Commission shall be fully associated in the tasks referred to in paragraphs 1 and 2. The Presidency shall be assisted in those tasks if need be by the next Member State to hold the Presidency.

(5) The Council may, whenever it deems it necessary, appoint a special representative with a mandate in relation to particular policy issues.

Article 19

(1) Member States shall coordinate their action in international organisations and at international conferences. They shall uphold the common positions in such fora. In international organisations and at international conferences where not all the Member States participate, those which do take part shall uphold the common positions.

(2) Without prejudice to paragraph 1 and Article 14 (3), Member States represented in international organisations or international conferences where not all the Member States participate shall keep the latter informed of any matter of common interest. Member States which are also members of the United Nations Security Council will concert and keep the other Member States fully informed. Member States which are permanent members of the Security Council will, in the execution of their functions, ensure the defence of the positions and the interests of the Union, without prejudice to their responsibilities under the provisions of the United Nations Charter.

Article 20

The diplomatic and consular missions of the Member States and the Commission Delegations in third countries and international conferences, and their representations to international organisations, shall cooperate in ensuring that the common positions and joint actions adopted by the Council are complied with and implemented.

They shall step up cooperation by exchanging information, carrying out joint assessments and contributing to the implementation of the provisions referred to in Article 8c of the Treaty establishing the European Community.

Article 21

The Presidency shall consult the European Parliament on the main aspects and the basic choices of the common foreign and security policy and shall ensure that the views of the European Parliament are duly taken into consideration. The European Parliament shall be kept regularly informed by the Presidency and the Commission of the development of the Union's foreign and security policy.

The European Parliament may ask questions of the Council or make recommendations to it. It shall hold an annual debate on progress in implementing the common foreign and security policy.

Article 22

(1)   Any Member State or the Commission may refer to the Council any question relating to the common foreign and security policy and may submit proposals to the Council.

(2)   In cases requiring a rapid decision, the Presidency, of its own motion, or at the request of the Commission or a Member State, shall convene an extraordinary Council meeting within forty-eight hours or, in an emergency, within a shorter period.

Article 23

(1)   Decisions under this Title shall be taken by the Council acting unanimously. Abstentions by members present in person or represented shall not prevent the adoption of such decisions.

(2)   When abstaining in a vote, any member of the Council may qualify its abstention by making a formal declaration under the present subparagraph. In that case, it shall not be obliged to apply the decision, but shall accept that the decision commits the Union. In a spirit of mutual solidarity, the Member State concerned shall refrain from any action likely to conflict with or impede Union action based on that decision and the other Member States shall respect its position. If the members of the Council qualifying their abstention in this way represent more than one third of the votes weighted in accordance with Article 148(2) of the Treaty establishing the European Community, the decision shall not be adopted.

(3)   By derogation from the provisions of paragraph 1, the Council shall act by qualified majority:

–   when adopting joint actions, common positions or taking any other decision on the basis of a common strategy;
–   when adopting any decision implementing a joint action or a common position.

If a member of the Council declares that, for important and stated reasons of national policy, it intends to oppose the adoption of a decision to be taken by qualified majority, a vote shall not be taken. The Council may, acting by a qualified majority, request that the matter be referred to the European Council for decision by unanimity.

The votes of the members of the Council shall be weighted in accordance with Article 148(2) of the Treaty establishing the European Community. For their adoption, decisions shall require at least 62 votes in favour, cast by at least 10 members.

This paragraph shall not apply to decisions having military or defence implications.

For procedural questions, the Council shall act by a majority of its members.

Article 24

When it is necessary to conclude an agreement with one or more States or international organisations in implementation of this Title, the Council, acting unanimously, may authorise the Presidency, assisted by the Commission as appropriate, to open negotiations to that effect. Such agreements shall be concluded by the Council acting unanimously on a recommendation from the Presidency. No agreement shall be binding on a Member State whose representative in the Council states that it has to comply with the requirements of its own constitutional procedure; the other members of the Council may agree that the agreement shall apply provisionally to them.

The provisions of this Article shall also apply to matters falling under Title VI.

Article 25

Without prejudice to Article 151 of the Treaty establishing the European Community, a Political Committee shall monitor the international situation in the areas covered by the common foreign and security policy and contribute to the definition of policies by delivering opinions to the Council at the request of the Council or on its own initiative. It shall also monitor the implementation of agreed policies, without prejudice to the responsibility of the Presidency and the Commission.

Article 26

The Secretary-General of the Council, High Representative for the common foreign and security policy, shall assist the Council in matters coming within the scope of the common foreign and security policy, in particular through contributing to the formulation, preparation and implementation of policy decisions, and, when appropriate and acting on behalf of the Council at the request of the Presidency, through conducting political dialogue with third parties.

Article 27

The Commission shall be fully associated with the work carried out in the common foreign and security policy field.

Article 28

(1)   Articles 137, 138, 139 to 142, 146, 147, 150 to 153, 157 to 163, 191a and 217 of the Treaty establishing the European Community shall apply to the provisions relating to the areas referred to in this Title.

(2)   Administrative expenditure which the provisions relating to the areas referred to in this Title entail for the institutions shall be charged to the budget of the European Communities.

(3)   Operational expenditure to which the implementation of those provisions gives rise shall also be charged to the budget of the European Communities, except for such expenditure arising from operations having military or defence implications and cases where the Council acting unanimously decides otherwise. In cases where expenditure is not charged to the budget of the European Communities it shall be charged to the Member States in accordance with the gross national product scale, unless the Council acting unanimously decides otherwise. As for expenditure arising from operations having military or defence implications, Member States whose representatives in the Council have made a formal declaration under Article 23(1), second subparagraph, shall not be obliged to contribute to the financing thereof.

(4)   The budgetary procedure laid down in the Treaty establishing the European Community shall apply to the expenditure charged to the budget of the European Communities.'

Appendix 2

Treaty of Amsterdam: Declaration relating to the Western European Union

The Conference notes the following Declaration, adopted by the Council of Ministers of the Western European Union on 22 July 1997

'DECLARATION OF WESTERN EUROPEAN UNION ON THE ROLE OF WESTERN EUROPEAN UNION AND ITS RELATIONS WITH THE EUROPEAN UNION AND WITH THE ATLANTIC ALLIANCE'

INTRODUCTION

The Western European Union (WEU) Member States agreed at Maastricht in 1991 on the need to develop a genuine European Security and Defence Identity (ESDI) and to assume a greater European responsibility for defence matters. In the light of the Treaty of Amsterdam, they reaffirm the importance of continuing and strengthening these efforts. WEU is an integral part of the development of the European Union (EU) providing the Union with access to an operational capability, notably in the context of the Petersberg tasks and is an essential element of the development of the ESDI within the Atlantic Alliance in accordance with the Paris Declaration and with the decisions taken by NATO ministers in Berlin.

Today the WEU Council brings together all the Member States of the European Union and all the European Members of the Atlantic Alliance in accordance with their respective status. The Council also brings together those States with the Central and Eastern European States linked to the European Union by an Association Agreement and that are applicants for accession to both the European Union and the Atlantic Alliance. WEU is thus establishing itself as a genuine framework for dialogue and cooperation among Europeans on wider European security and defence issues.

The European Union shall draw up, together with the Western European Union, arrangements for enhanced cooperation between them, within a year from the entry into force of the Treaty of Amsterdam.'

WEU's RELATIONS WITH THE EUROPEAN UNION: ACCOMPANYING THE
IMPLEMENTATION OF THE TREATY OF AMSTERDAM

In the 'Declaration on the Role of the Western European Union and its Relations
with the European Union and with the Atlantic Alliance' of 10 December 1991,
WEU Member States set as their objective 'to build up WEU in stages as the
defence component of the European Union'.

They today reaffirm this aim as developed by the Treaty of Amsterdam.

When the Union avails itself of WEU, WEU will elaborate and implement decisions
and actions of the EU which have defence implications. In elaborating and implementing decisions and actions of the EU for which the Union avails itself of WEU,
WEU will act consistently with guidelines established by the European Council.

WEU supports the Union in framing the defence aspects of the European Union
Common Foreign and Security Policy as set out in Article 17 of the Treaty on
European Union.

WEU confirms that when the European Union avails itself of WEU to elaborate and
implement decisions of the Union on the tasks referred to in Article 17(2) of the
Treaty on European Union, all Member States of the Union shall be entitled to
participate fully in the tasks in question in accordance with Article 17(3) of the
Treaty on European Union.

WEU will develop the role of the Observers in WEU in line with provisions
contained in Article 17(3) and will adopt the necessary practical arrangements to
allow all Member States of the EU contributing to the tasks undertaken by WEU at
the request of the EU to participate fully and on an equal footing in planning and
decision-taking in the WEU.

Consistent with the Protocol on Article 17 of the Treaty on European Union, WEU
shall draw up, together with the European Union, arrangements for enhanced cooperation between them. In this regard, a range of measures, on some of which
work is already in hand in WEU, can be taken forward now, such as:

*   arrangements for improving the coordination of the consultation and decision-
    making processes of the respective Organisations, in particular in crisis
    situations;
*   holding of joint meetings of the relevant bodies of the two Organisations;
*   harmonisation as much as possible of the sequence of the Presidencies of WEU
    and the EU, as well as the administrative rules and practices of the two
    Organisations;
*   close coordination of the work of the staff of the Secretariat-General of the
    WEU and the General Secretariat of the Council of the EU, including through
    the exchange and secondment of personnel;

- arrangements to allow the relevant bodies of the EU, including its Policy Planning and Early Warning Unit, to draw on the resources of WEU's Planning Cell, Situation Centre and Satellite Centre;
- cooperation in the field of armaments, as appropriate, within the framework of the Western European Armaments Group (WEAG), as the European forum for armaments cooperation, the EU and WEU in the context of rationalisation of the European armaments market and the establishment of a European Armaments Agency;
- practical arrangements for ensuring cooperation with the European Commission reflecting its role in the CFSP as defined in the revised Treaty on European Union;
- improved security arrangements with the European Union.

RELATIONS BETWEEN WEU AND NATO IN THE FRAMEWORK OF THE DEVELOPMENT OF AN ESDI WITHIN THE ATLANTIC ALLIANCE

The Atlantic Alliance continues to be the basis of collective defence under the North Atlantic Treaty. It remains the essential forum for consultation among Allies and the framework in which they agree on policies bearing on their security and defence commitments under the Washington Treaty. The Alliance has embarked on a process of adaptation and reform so that it can more effectively carry out the full range of its missions. This process is aimed at strengthening and renewing the transatlantic partnership, including building an ESDI within the Alliance.

WEU is an essential element of the development of the European Security and Defence Identity within the Atlantic Alliance and will accordingly continue its efforts to strengthen institutional and practical cooperation with NATO.

In addition to its support for the common defence enshrined in Article 5 of the Washington Treaty and Article V of the modified Brussels Treaty, WEU takes an active role in conflict prevention and crisis management as provided for in the Petersberg Declaration. In this context, WEU undertakes to perform its role to the full, respecting the full transparency and complementarity between the two Organisations.

WEU affirms that this identity will be grounded on sound military principles and supported by appropriate military planning and will permit the creation of militarily coherent and effective forces capable of operating under the political control and strategic direction of WEU.

To this end, WEU will develop its cooperation with NATO, in particular in the following fields:

- mechanisms for consultation between WEU and NATO in the context of a crisis;
- WEU's active involvement in the NATO defence planning process;

- operational links between WEU and NATO for the planning, preparation and conduct of operations using NATO assets and capabilities under the political control and strategic direction of WEU, including:
  * military planning, conducted by NATO in coordination with WEU, and exercises;
  * a framework agreement on the transfer, monitoring and return of NATO assets and capabilities;
  * liaison between WEU and NATO in the context of European command arrangements.

This cooperation will continue to evolve, also taking account of the adaptation of the Alliance.

WEU's OPERATIONAL ROLE IN THE DEVELOPMENT OF THE ESDI

WEU will develop its role as the European politico-military body for crisis management, by using the assets and capabilities made available by WEU nations on a national or multinational basis, and having recourse, when appropriate, to NATO's assets and capabilities under arrangements being worked out. In this context, WEU will also support the UN and OSCE in their crisis management tasks.

WEU will contribute, in the framework of Article 17 of the Treaty on European Union, to the progressive framing of a common defence policy and carry forward its concrete implementation through the further development of its own operational role.

To this end, WEU will take forward work in the following fields:

- WEU has developed crisis management mechanisms and procedures which will be updated as WEU gains experience through exercises and operations. The implementation of Petersberg missions calls for flexible modes of action geared to the diversity of crisis situations and making optimum use of the available capabilities including through recourse to a national headquarters, which might be one provided by a framework nation, or to a multinational headquarters answerable to WEU or to NATO assets and capabilities;
- WEU has already worked out Preliminary Conclusions on the Formulation of a Common European Defence Policy which is an initial contribution on the objectives, scope and means of a common European defence policy.
- WEU will continue this work on the basis in particular of the Paris Declaration and taking account of the relevant elements of the decisions of WEU and NATO summits and ministerial meetings since Birmingham. It will focus on the following fields:
  * definition of principles for the use of armed forces of the WEU States for WEU Petersberg operations in pursuit of common European security interests;
  * organisation of operational means for Petersberg tasks, such as generic and contingency planning and exercising, preparation and interoperability of

forces, including through participation in the NATO defence planning process, as appropriate;
* strategic mobility on the basis of its current work;
* defence intelligence, through its Planning Cell, Situation Centre and Satellite Centre;
• WEU has adopted many measures to strengthen its operational role (Planning Cell, Situation Centre, Satellite Centre). The improvement of the functioning of the military components at WEU Headquarters and the establishment, under the Council's authority, of a military committee will represent a further enhancement of structures which are important for the successful preparation and conduct of WEU operations; with the aim of opening participation in all its operations to Associate Members and Observer States, WEU will also examine the necessary modalities to allow Associate Members and Observer States to participate fully in accordance with their status in all operations undertaken by WEU;
• WEU recalls that Associate Members take part on the same basis as full members in operations to which they contribute, as well as in relevant exercises and planning. WEU will also examine the question of participation of the Observers as fully as possible in accordance with their status in planning and decision-taking within WEU in all operations to which they contribute;
• WEU will, in consultation where appropriate with the relevant bodies, examine the possibilities for maximum participation in its activities by Associate Members and Observer States in accordance with their status. It will address in particular activities in the fields of armaments, space and military studies;
• WEU will examine how to strengthen the Associate Partners' participation in an increasing number of activities.'

Appendix 3

Membership of the WEU (1999)

- 10 Member States (members of both the European Union and NATO): Belgium, France, Germany, Greece, Italy, Luxembourg, the Netherlands, Portugal, Spain and the United Kingdom;

- 6 Associate Members (also members of NATO): Hungary, Iceland, Norway, Poland, Czech Republic and Turkey;

- 5 Observers (also members of the EU): Austria, Denmark, Finland, Ireland and Sweden, i.e. four neutral countries and one NATO member, Denmark, which is not a full member of WEU;

- 7 Associate Partners (as against 10 previously), all signatories of a Europe Agreement with the EU: Bulgaria, Estonia, Latvia, Lithuania, Romania, Slovakia and Slovenia.

Appendix 4

Amsterdam Declaration on the Establishment of a
Policy Planning and Early Warning Unit

The Conference agrees that:

1. A policy planning and early warning unit shall be established in the General Secretariat of the Council under the responsibility of its Secretary-General, High Representative for the CFSP. Appropriate cooperation shall be established with the Commission in order to ensure full coherence with the Union's external economic and development policies.

2. The tasks of the unit shall include the following:

    (a) monitoring and analysing developments in areas relevant to the CFSP;

    (b) providing assessments of the Union's foreign and security policy interests and identifying areas where the CFSP could focus in future;

    (c) providing timely assessments and early warning of events or situations which may have significant repercussions for the Union's foreign and security policy, including potential political crises;

    (d) producing, at the request of either the Council or the Presidency or on its own initiative, argued policy options papers to be presented under the responsibility of the Presidency as a contribution to policy formulation in the Council, and which may contain analyses, recommendations and strategies for the CFSP.

The unit shall consist of personnel drawn from the General Secretariat, the Member States, the Commission and the WEU.

Any Member State or the Commission may make suggestions to the unit for work to be undertaken.

Member States and the Commission shall assist the policy planning process by providing, to the fullest extent possible, relevant information, including confidential information.

Appendix 5

Cologne European Council Declaration on Strengthening the Common European Policy on Security and Defence

1. We, the members of the European Council, are resolved that the European Union shall play its full role on the international stage. To that end, we intend to give the European Union the necessary means and capabilities to assume its responsibilities regarding a common European policy on security and defence. The work undertaken on the initiative of the German Presidency and the entry into force of the Treaty of Amsterdam permit us today to take a decisive step forward.

   In pursuit of our Common Foreign and Security Policy objectives and the progressive framing of a common defence policy, we are convinced that the Council should have the ability to take decisions on the full range of conflict prevention and crisis management tasks defined in the Treaty on European Union, the 'Petersberg tasks'. To this end, the Union must have the capacity for autonomous action, backed up by credible military forces, the means to decide to use them, and a readiness to do so, in order to respond to international crises without prejudice to actions by NATO. The EU will thereby increase its ability to contribute to international peace and security in accordance with the principles of the UN Charter.

2. We are convinced that to fully assume its tasks in the field of conflict prevention and crisis management the European Union must have at its disposal the appropriate capabilities and instruments. We therefore commit ourselves to further develop more effective European military capabilities from the basis of existing national, bi-national and multinational capabilities and to strengthen our own capabilities for that purpose. This requires the maintenance of a sustained defence effort, the implementation of the necessary adaptations and notably the reinforcement of our capabilities in the field of intelligence, strategic transport, command and control. This also requires efforts to adapt, exercise and bring together national and multinational European forces.

We also recognise the need to undertake sustained efforts to strengthen the industrial and technological defence base, which we want to be competitive and dynamic. We are determined to foster the restructuring of the European defence industries amongst those States involved. With industry we will therefore work towards closer and more efficient defence industry collaboration. We will seek further progress in the harmonisation of military requirements and the planning and procurement of arms, as Member States consider appropriate.

3. We welcome the results of the NATO Washington summit as regards NATO support for the process launched by the EU and its confirmation that a more effective role for the European Union in conflict prevention and crisis management will contribute to the vitality of a renewed Alliance. In implementing this process launched by the EU, we shall ensure the development of effective mutual consultation, cooperation and transparency between the European Union and NATO.

We want to develop an effective EU-led crisis management in which NATO members, as well as neutral and non-allied members, of the EU can participate fully and on an equal footing in the EU operations.

We will put in place arrangements that allow non-EU European allies and partners to take part to the fullest possible extent in this endeavour.

4. We therefore approve and adopt the report prepared by the German Presidency, which reflects the consensus among the Member States.

5. We are now determined to launch a new step in the construction of the European Union. To this end we task the General Affairs Council to prepare the conditions and the measures necessary to achieve these objectives, including the definition of the modalities for the inclusion of those functions of the WEU which will be necessary for the EU to fulfil its new responsibilities in the area of the Petersberg tasks. In this regard, our aim is to take the necessary decisions by the end of the year 2000. In that event, the WEU as an organisation would have completed its purpose. The different status of Member States with regard to collective defence guarantees will not be affected. The Alliance remains the foundation of the collective defence of its Member States.

We therefore invite the Finnish Presidency to take the work forward within the General Affairs Council on the basis of this declaration and the report of the Presidency to the European Council meeting in Cologne. We look forward to a progress report by the Finnish Presidency to the Helsinki European Council meeting.

Appendix 6

Presidency Report on Strengthening of the
Common European Policy on Security and Defence

1.   Introduction

The Treaty of Amsterdam which entered into force on 1 May provides for the enhancement of the Common Foreign and Security Policy (CFSP), including the progressive framing of a common defence policy as provided in Article 17 of the TEU. The Treaty also provides for the possibility of integrating the WEU into the EU, should the European Council so decide.

The European Council in Vienna welcomed the new impetus given to the debate on a common European policy in security and defence. It considered that in order for the EU to be in a position to play its full role on the international stage, the CFSP must be backed by credible operational capabilities. Furthermore, it welcomed the Franco-British declaration made on 4 December 1998 in St. Malo. The European Council invited the German Presidency to pursue this debate and agreed to examine the question again at the European Council in Cologne. To this end Foreign Ministers discussed the subject at their informal meeting in Reinhartshausen on 13/14 March and at the General Affairs Council on 17 May.

The NATO Washington Summit welcomed the new impetus given to the strengthening of a common European policy on security and defence by the Amsterdam Treaty and confirmed that a stronger European role will help contribute to the vitality of the Alliance for the 21st century. The NATO summit furthermore stressed that the development of a CFSP, as called for in the Amsterdam Treaty, would be compatible with the common security and defence policy established within the framework of the Washington Treaty. This process will lead to more complementarity, cooperation and synergy.

At the WEU Ministerial Council on 10 and 11 May this question was also discussed on the basis of the informal reflection which was initiated at the Rome Ministerial Council. Member States will undertake efforts in line with the conclusions of the ongoing WEU Audit of European defence capabilities.

2.   Guiding Principles

The aim is to strengthen the CFSP by the development of a common European policy on security and defence. This requires a capacity for autonomous action backed up by credible military capabilities and appropriate decision making bodies. Decisions to act would be taken within the framework of the CFSP according to appropriate procedures in order to reflect the specific nature of decisions in this field. The Council of the European Union would thus be able to take decisions on the whole range of political, economic and military instruments at its disposal when responding to crisis situations. The European Union is committed to preserve peace and strengthen international security in accordance with the principles of the UN Charter as well as the principles of the Helsinki Final Act and the objectives of the Charter of Paris, as provided for in Article 11 of the TEU.

The Amsterdam Treaty incorporates the Petersberg tasks ('humanitarian and rescue tasks, peace-keeping tasks and tasks of combat forces in crisis management, including peace-making') into the Treaty.

The focus of our efforts therefore would be to assure that the European Union has at its disposal the necessary capabilities (including military capabilities) and appropriate structures for effective EU decision making in crisis management within the scope of the Petersberg tasks. This is the area where a European capacity to act is required most urgently. The development of an EU military crisis management capacity is to be seen as an activity within the framework of the CFSP (Title V of the TEU) and as a part of the progressive framing of a common defence policy in accordance with Article 17 of the TEU.

The Atlantic Alliance remains the foundation of the collective defence of its Members. The commitments under Article 5 of the Washington Treaty and Article V of the Brussels Treaty will in any event be preserved for the Member States party to these Treaties. The policy of the Union shall not prejudice the specific character of the security and defence policy of certain Member States.

3.   Decision Making

As regards EU decision making in the field of security and defence policy, necessary arrangements must be made in order to ensure political control and strategic direction of EU-led Petersberg operations so that the EU can decide and conduct such operations effectively.

Furthermore, the EU will need a capacity for analysis of situations, sources of intelligence, and a capability for relevant strategic planning.

This may require in particular:

–   regular (or ad hoc) meetings of the General Affairs Council, as appropriate including Defence Ministers;

- a permanent body in Brussels (Political and Security Committee) consisting of representatives with political/military expertise;
- an EU Military Committee consisting of Military Representatives making recommendations to the Political and Security Committee;
- a EU Military Staff including a Situation Centre;
- other resources such as a Satellite Centre, Institute for Security Studies.

Further institutional questions may need to be addressed.

Decisions relating to crisis management tasks, in particular decisions having military or defence implications will be taken in accordance with Article 23 of the Treaty on European Union. Member States will retain in all circumstances the right to decide if and when their national forces are deployed.

4.   Implementation

As regards military capabilities, Member States need to develop further forces (including headquarters) that are suited also to crisis management operations, without any unnecessary duplication. The main characteristics include: deployability, sustainability, interoperability, flexibility and mobility.

For the effective implementation of EU-led operations the European Union will have to determine, according to the requirements of the case, whether it will conduct:

- EU-led operations using NATO assets and capabilities or
- EU-led operations without recourse to NATO assets and capabilities.

For EU-led operations without recourse to NATO assets and capabilities, the EU could use national or multinational European means pre-identified by Member States. This will require either the use of national command structures providing multinational representation in headquarters or drawing on existing command structures within multinational forces. Further arrangements to enhance the capacity of European multinational and national forces to respond to crises situations will be needed.

For EU-led operations having recourse to NATO assets and capabilities, including European command arrangements, the main focus should be on the following aspects:

- Implementation of the arrangements based on the Berlin decisions of 1996 and the Washington NATO summit decisions of April 1999.
- The further arrangements set out by NATO at its summit meeting in Washington should address in particular:
    = assured EU access to NATO planning capabilities able to contribute to military planing for EU-led operations;
    = the presumption of availability to the EU of pre-identified NATO capabilities and common assets for use in EU-led operations.

5.   Modalities of participation and cooperation

The successful creation of a European policy on security and defence will require in particular:

–   the possibility of all EU Member States, including non-allied members, to participate fully and on an equal footing in EU operations;

–   satisfactory arrangements for European NATO members who are not EU Member States to ensure their fullest possible involvement in EU-led operations, building on existing consultation arrangements within WEU;

–   arrangements to ensure that all participants in an EU-led operation will have equal rights in respect of the conduct of that operation, without prejudice to the principle of the EU's decision-making autonomy, notably the right of the Council to discuss and decide matters of principle and policy;

–   the need to ensure the development of effective mutual consultation, cooperation and transparency between NATO and the EU;

–   the consideration of ways to ensure the possibility for WEU Associate Partners to be involved.

Appendix 7

Size of Armed Forces of Member States and other Countries

Armed Forces of EU Member States

Country	Total	Army	Navy	Airforce
Austria	45,500	41,250	-	4,250
Belgium	43,700	28,250	2,600	11,600
Denmark	32,100	22,900	3,700	5,500
Finland	31,700	24,000	5,000	2,700
France	358,800	203,200	63,300	78,100
Germany	333,500	230,600	26,700	76,200
Greece	168,500	116,000	19,500	33,000
Ireland	11,500	9,300	1,100	1,100
Italy	298,400	165,500	40,000	63,600
Luxembourg	811	811	-	-
Netherlands	57,180	27,000	13,800	11,980
Portugal	53,600	24,800	16,850	7,300
Spain	193,950	127,000	36,950	30,000
Sweden	53,100	35,100	9,200	8,800
United Kingdom	210,940	113,900	44,500	52,540

Armed Forces of Candidate Countries

Country	Total	Army	Navy	Airforce
Bulgaria	101,500	50,400	6,100	19,300
Czech Republic	59,100	25,300	-	15,000
Estonia	4,340	3,980	320	36
Hungary	43,300	23,400	290	11,500
Latvia	4,960	2,350	880	130
Lithuania	11,130	6,750	1,320	970
Poland	240,650	142,500	17,100	55,300
Romania	219,650	11,300	22,100	46,300
Slovak Republic	45,450	23,800	-	12,000
Slovenia	9,550	9,550	-	8
Cyprus	10,000	10,000	-	-
Malta	1,900	1,900	-	-
Turkey	639,000	525,000	51,000	63,000

Armed Forces of Other Countries

Country	Total	Army	Navy	Airforce
US	1,401,600	479,400	380,600	370,300
Russia	1,159,000	420,000	180,000	210,000
Ukraine	346,400	171,300	12,500	124,400
Belarus	83,000	43,000	22,000	-
Yugoslavia	114,200	90,000	7,500	16,700

Note: These figures should be interpreted with care as they do not give any breakdown of the military formations, training, equipment, etc, of the various countries, The real issue for the EU is capabilities and this will require considerable restructuring of the Member States' armed forces.

Source: Military Balance, 1999, International Institute of Strategic Studies, London.

Glossary

CFSP Counsellors. These are officials based in the Permanent Representations of Member States in Brussels and the Commission. They examine horizontal problems concerning CFSP, in particular legal, institutional and financial aspects of CFSP actions (notably Joint Actions, Common Positions) which they finalise before approval by Coreper and the Council. Tasks include strengthening coherence between CFSP and EC external action and more specific issues (economic sanctions, financing). They assist both the Political Committee and Coreper. Meetings are convened by the Presidency as necessary (usually once a week).

Committee of Permanent Representatives ('Coreper'). Permanent Representatives of Member States to the EU and the Commission Deputy Secretary General meet once a week to prepare Council meetings and decisions, including those related to the General Affairs Council and CFSP. Coreper has overall responsibility for preparing the work of the Council in all its compositions. This means that all items submitted to the Council must previously have been placed on the agenda of Coreper, which, if need arises, endeavours, at its level, to reach an agreement to be submitted for adoption by the Council (Coreper can attach comments and recommendations to opinions submitted to the Council by the Political Committee).

Common position is designed to make cooperation more systematic and improve its coordination. The Member States are required to comply with and uphold such positions which have been adopted unanimously at Council meetings.

Common strategy is a new instrument. The European Council will define the principles and general guidelines for the CFSP and decide on common strategies to be implemented by the Union in fields where the Member States have important interests in common.

COREU Telex Network. The COREU telex network (Correspondance européenne) is a network allowing transmission of enciphered messages used for all aspects of information exchange between capitals and with the Commission, and by the Presidency in the everyday management of CFSP. The Council may act on CFSP matters by simplified written procedure using the COREU network.

Council CFSP Working Groups. CFSP working groups (or parties) are composed of experts from EU Member States and the Commission meeting along geographical and horizontal lines to elaborate policy documents and options for the consideration of the Political Committee (list of groups in annex). Some of these groups are 'merged' (to cover both 'pillars' I and II) but still operate according to the presence of 'CFSP officials' from capitals (meaning that the groups only operate as real merged groups about once a month). Merged groups report both to the Political Committee and Coreper.

The tasks of the merged group meetings include elaboration of: (a) joint analysis of a third country situation or multilateral question, and the joint position which might be adopted by the European Union, (b) proposals for approval by the Political Committee as measures for implementing the CFSP (approaches, requests to be addressed to the EU representations in third countries and other preparatory measures, statements by the Presidency on behalf of the European Union and (c) recommendations for further Council initiatives in the area of CFSP (which, if decided by the Political Committee, may be presented as an opinion by that Committee to the Council) and for the political follow-up to such initiatives.

Council of Ministers. EU Foreign Ministers meet at least once a month as the General Affairs Council (GAC) in which the Commission is represented by the competent Commissioner in charge of external relations. According to the Treaty (Art. 13) the Council 'shall take the decisions necessary for defining and implementing' the CFSP 'on the basis of the general guidelines defined by the European Council', it 'shall recommend Common Strategies to the European Council and implement these, in particular by adopting joint actions and common positions' and 'ensure the unity, consistency and effectiveness of action by the Union' in the field of CFSP. The Council is the general forum for information and consultation on CFSP matters among Member States (Art. 16 TEU). In addition to its permanent role in ensuring the smooth operation of the Community and the Union and its specific responsibility under CFSP, the GAC has overall responsibility for all preparatory work for the European Council; consequently matters to be submitted to the European Council must first be submitted to the GAC. The Council and the Commission are jointly responsible for 'the consistency of the Union's external activities as a whole in the context of its external relations, security, economic and development policies' and 'shall co-operate to this end' (Art. 3 TEU).

Declaration. This is an instrument for which there is no provision in Title V of the Treaty on European Union but which was a feature of European political cooperation (EPC). It is not a mandatory instrument and is still frequently used under the CFSP.

European Correspondents. European Correspondents of Member States and the Commission ensure coordination of the input of the Member State or of the Commission in the machinery and procedures of CFSP. They assist the Political Directors and prepare and participate in meetings within the CFSP structures, including the Political Committee and political dialogue meetings with third countries. In the Political Committee, the European Correspondents meet before the Political Directors to handle certain agenda points and examine working group reports that do not need to be discussed at the level of Political Directors. In addition European Correspondents coordinate daily CFSP communications, notably through the COREU network (see above).

European Council. The European Council is composed of Heads of State and Government and the Commission President who meet at least once every half year. It 'shall provide the Union with the necessary impetus for its development and shall define the general policy guidelines thereof' (Art. 4 TEU). In CFSP in particular, its role is to 'define the principles and general guidelines…including for matters with defence implications' (Art. 13 TEU). Furthermore the European Council is 'to decide on common strategies to be implemented by the Union in areas where the Member States have important interests in common'. The direct involvement of the European Council in CFSP adds political weight and commits the highest political authorities in Member States to the CFSP.

European Parliament. The European Parliament is consulted and kept informed regularly. According to the Treaty (Art. 21) 'The Presidency shall consult the European Parliament on the main aspects and the basic choices of the common foreign and security policy and shall ensure that the views of the European Parliament are duly taken into consideration. The European Parliament shall be kept regularly informed by the Presidency and the Commission of the development of the Union's foreign and security policy. The European Parliament may ask questions of the Council or make recommendations to it. It shall hold an annual debate on progress in implementing the common foreign and security policy.' According to the Inter-institutional Agreement between Parliament, Council and Commission on CFSP financing, the Presidency shall, on a yearly basis, consult the Parliament on a document established by the Council on the main aspects and basic choices on CFSP, including the financial implications for the Community budget. The Presidency and/or the Commission, when considered useful and necessary, attends the meetings of Parliament's Committee on Foreign Affairs and Security and participates, if need be, in Parliament's debates in plenary session. At Council meetings the Presidency informs the Council of Parliament's reactions, communications, questions, recommendations or resolutions concerning CFSP.

High Representative (Mr CFSP). The Amsterdam Treaty introduces the new office of a High Representative (HR) for CFSP. He will be the Council Secretary General. The HR 'shall assist the Council in matters coming within the scope of the CFSP, in particular through contributing to the formulation, preparation and implementation of policy decisions, and, when appropriate and acting on behalf of the Council at the request of the Presidency, through conducting political dialogue with third countries' (Art. 26). The HR will also 'assist the Presidency' in the external representation of the EU and in the implementation of decisions in CFSP matters (Art. 18).

Joint action refers to a legal instrument under Title V of the Treaty on European Union, means coordinated action by the Member States whereby resources of all kinds (human resources, know-how, financing, equipment and so on) are mobilized to attain specific objectives fixed by the Council on the base of general guidelines from the European Council.

Petersberg Tasks. The Petersberg Declaration of 19 June 1992 underlined the determination to develop the Western European Union (WEU) as the EU´s defence component and as a means of strengthening the European pillar of the Atlantic Alliance (NATO). The three parts of the declaration define the guidelines for the future development of the WEU. WEU Member States declare their readiness to make available military units from the whole spectrum of their conventional armed forces for military tasks conducted under the authority of WEU. The different types of military tasks which WEU might undertake were defined: apart from contributing to the common defence in accordance with Article 5 of the Washington Treaty and Article V of the modified Brussels Treaty, military units of WEU Member States could be employed for: humanitarian and rescue tasks; peace-keeping tasks; tasks of combat forces in crisis management, including peacemaking. These 'Petersberg tasks' are specifically included in a new Article of the Treaty on European Union, which replaced Article 14. The Petersberg Declaration also states that WEU is prepared to support, on a case-by-case basis and in accordance with its own procedures, the effective implementation of conflict-prevention and crisis-management measures, including peacekeeping activities of the CSCE (now OSCE) or the United Nations Security Council. At the same time, the Declaration supports a solid transatlantic partnership and stresses the importance of implementing the Declaration on WEU (No. 30) annexed to the Maastricht Treaty. The third part of the Declaration relates to the enlargement of the WEU: in it the Member States define the rights and obligations of other European states belonging to the European Union and the Atlantic Alliance as future members, observers or associate members.

Policy Planning and Early Warning Unit (PPEWU). In accordance with Declaration 6 (see Appendix 4), a Policy Planning and Early Warning Unit (PPEWU) is established within the Council Secretariat and under the responsibility of the Council Secretary General (High Representative). Its mandate includes monitoring, analysis and assessment of international developments and events, including early warning on potential crises. It also includes drafting, upon Council request or on its own initiative, of policy options which may contain recommendations and strategies for presentation to the Council under the responsibility of the Presidency as a contribution to policy formulation. PPEWU staff will come from the Council Secretariat General, Member States, the Commission and the WEU.

Political Committee. The Political Committee is composed of the Political Directors of Member States and the Commission. According to the Treaty (Art. 25) their main tasks include: (a) monitoring the international situation in the areas covered by the CFSP, (b) contributing to the definition of policies by delivering opinions to the Council at the request of the Council or on its own initiative, and (c) monitoring the implementation of agreed policies, 'without prejudice to the responsibility of the Presidency and the Commission'.

The Committee meets about twice a month and usually in the margins of the

General Affairs Council in order to make final preparations of CFSP decisions in light of latest developments. The possibility for the Committee to meet more frequently was spelled out in a declaration on Article 25 of the Amsterdam Treaty (declaration No. 5 annexed to the Final Act) which states that 'Member States shall ensure that the Political Committee' is able to meet 'at any time, in the event of international crises or other urgent matters, at very short notice at Political Director or deputy level'.

Presidency/Troika. The Amsterdam Treaty modifies rules on external representation and responsibility for implementation of decisions in the area of CFSP. The Presidency remains in charge and represents the Union in matters coming within CFSP, as well as being responsible for implementation of decisions. In its tasks it will be assisted from now on by the Secretary General of the Council as High Representative for CFSP and 'if need be' by the next Member State to hold the Presidency. As before, the Commission will be fully associated in these tasks.

Western European Union (WEU) is an organization which was set up in 1948 for the purposes of cooperation on defence and security. It consists of the Member States of the EU (except Austria, Denmark, Finland, Ireland and Sweden, which have observer status). Iceland, Norway and Turkey are associated States. The Treaty on European Union raised WEU to the rank of an 'integral part of the development of the Union', while preserving its institutional autonomy, and gave it the task of elaborating and implementing decisions and actions which had defence implications.

Ten Central and Eastern European countries enjoy the status of Associate Partner: Bulgaria, Hungary, Poland, the Czech Republic, Romania, the Slovak Republic, Slovenia and the three Baltic States. It allows them to attend meetings of the WEU Council, where they are kept regularly informed of the activities of the Council working groups; they may be invited to participate in these groups on an ad hoc basis. They also have a permanent liaison arrangement with the Planning Cell. Finally, they may be involved in decisions taken by the Member States on the tasks listed in the Petersberg Declaration: humanitarian and rescue tasks, peacekeeping tasks, and tasks of combat forces in crisis management including peacemaking.

Bibliography

Albright, Madeleine
    1998   'The Right Balance Will Secure NATO's Future', *Financial Times*, 1 December: 23.

Allen, David, and Christopher Hill
    1994   *The Changing Context of European Foreign Policy* (London: Routledge).

Allen, David, Reinhard Rummel and Wolfgang Wessels
    1992   *European Political Cooperation* (London: Butterworths).

Avery, Graham, and Fraser Cameron
    1998   *The Enlargement of the European Union* (Contemporary European Studies, 1; Sheffield: Sheffield Academic Press).

Bildt, Carl
    1998   *Peace Journey* (London: Weidenfeld & Nicholson).

Bloes, Robert
    1970   'Le Plan Fouchet', *Cahiers de Bruges* 2: 1-15.

Boyer, Yves
    1997   'European Defense and Nuclear Deterrence', *Asia-Pacific Review*.

Bronstone, Adam
    1997   *European Union: United States Security Relations, Transatlantic Tensions and the Theory of International Relations* (Basingstoke: Macmillan).

Buchan, David
    1993   *Europe: The Strange Superpower* (Aldershot: Dartmouth Publishing Company).

Bulmer, Simon, and William E. Paterson
    1996   'Germany in the European Union: Gentle Giant or Emergent Leader?', *International Affairs*.

Burghardt, Günter, and Gerd Tebbe
    1995   'Die Gemeinsame Aussen- und Sicherheitspolitik der Europäischen Union—rechtliche Struktur und politischer Prozess', *Europarecht* 1–2: 2-20.

Cafruny, Alan, and Patrick Peters
    1998   *The Union and the World: The Political Economy of a Common European Foreign Policy* (The Hague: Kluwer Law International).

Cameron, Fraser
    1995   'The European Union and the OSCE', in Michael Lukas (ed.), *The OSCE in the 1990s* (Frankfurt: Nomos Verlag): 41-55.
    1996   'Developing the Common Foreign and Security Policy of Europe', *Brassey's Defence Yearbook* (London).

1997   'European Security: A Commission Perspective', *Royal United Services Institute Journal*.

Carlsnaes, Walter
1994   *European Foreign Policy: The EC and Changing Perspectives in Europe* (London: Sage Publications).

Cloos, Jim
1994   *La traité de Maastricht* (Brussels: Breylant).

Cottey, Andrew (ed.)
1999   *Subregional Co-operation in the New Europe* (London: Macmillan).

Crowe, Brian
1998   'Some Reflections on the Common Foreign and Security Policy', *European Foreign Affairs Review* 3: 319-24.

De Gaulle, Charles
1971   *Memoirs of Hope, Renewal and Endeavour* (New York: Simon and Schuster).

De Schoutheete, Philippe
1997   'L'avenir de l'Union européenne', *Politique étrangère*, March: 16-25.

Deighton, Anne (ed.)
1997   *Western European Union 1954–1997* (Oxford: Oxford University Press).

Deutsch, Karl, et al.
1957   *Political Community and the North Atlantic Area* (Princeton: Princeton University Press).

Duff, Andrew
1997   *The Treaty of Amsterdam* (London: The Federal Trust).

Edwards, Geoffrey, and Alfred Pijpers (eds.)
1997   *The Politics of European Treaty Reform: The 1996 IGC and Beyond* (London: Pinter).

Edwards, Geoffrey and Simon Nutall
1994   'Common Foreign and Security Policy', in *Maastricht and Beyond: Building the European Union* (London: Routledge).

Eliassen, Kjell (ed.)
1998   *Foreign and Security Policy in the European Union* (London: Sage).

Eyskens, Mark, David Owen and Michel Rocard
1997   *L'Europe peut-elle prévenir les conflits?* (Brusells: Philip Morris Institute for Public Policy Research).

Flockhart, Trne (ed.)
1998   *From Vision to Reality: Implementing Europe's New Security Order* (Oxford: Westview).

Frellesen, Thomas, and Roy H. Ginsberg
1994   *EU–US Foreign Policy Co-operation in the 1990s* (Brussels: Centre for European Policy Studies).

Gardner, Anthony Laurence
1997   *A New Era in US–EU Relations? The Clinton Administration and the New Transatlantic Agenda* (Aldershot: Avebury).

Gasteyger, Curt
1996   *An Ambiguous Power: The European Union in a Changing World* (Gütersloh: Bertelsmann).

Ginsberg, Roy
    1989   *Foreign Policy Actions of the European Community* (Boulder: Lynne
                Riener).
Glenny, Misha
    1996   *The Fall of Yugoslavia: The Third Balkan War* (Harmondsworth: Penguin
                Books).
Gordon, Philip
    1997a   'Does the WEU Have a Role?', *The Washington Quarterly*, April.
    1997b   'Europe's Uncommon Foreign Policy', *Journal of International Security*.
Gourlay, Catriona
    1999   *The European Parliament's Role in Scrutinising Defence and Security:
                An Uncertain Future* (International Security Information Service, Briefing
                Paper, 2).
Hill, Christopher
    1983   *National Foreign Policies and European Political Cooperation* (London:
                Allen and Unwin).
    1992   'The Capability-Expectations Gap, or Conceptualizing Europe's Interna-
                tional Role', *Journal of Common Market Studies* 31.3: 305-28.
    1996   *The Actors in Europe's Foreign Policy* (London: Routledge).
    1997   *Paradoxes of European Foreign Policy: Convergence, Divergence and
                Dialectics: National Foreign Policies and the CFSP* (Florence: European
                University Institute).
Holbrooke, Richard
    1998   *To End a War* (New York: Random House).
Holland, Martin
    1995a   'Bridging the Capability–Expectations Gap: A Case Study of the CFSP
                Joint Action on South Africa', *Journal of Common Market Studies* 4.
    1995b   *European Union Common Foreign Policy from EPC to CFSP Joint
                Action and South Africa* (New York: St Martin's Press; Basingstoke:
                Macmillan).
Holland, Martin (ed.)
    1997   *Common Foreign and Security Policy: The Record and Reforms* (London:
                Pinter).
Hurd, Douglas
    1994   'Developing the Common Foreign and Security Policy', *International
                Affairs*, 70.3.
    1997   *The Search for Peace* (London: Little, Brown & Co.).
Ischinger, Wolfgang
    1998   'Die gemeinsame Außen- und Sicherheitspolitik der Europäischen Union.
                Europäische Sicherheitsarchitektur im Aufbau', *Europäische Sicherheit* 2:
                47-63.
Janning, Josef
    1994   *Aussen- und Sicherheitspolitik nach Maastricht* (Gütersloh: Bertelsmann).
Jones, Robert
    1998   'Forging the European Union's CFSP', paper presented at UACES
                conference, 'Future of Europe', Glasgow, January 1999.

Keatinge, Patrick
    1996   *European Security: Ireland's Choices* (Dublin: Irish Institute of European Affairs).
Kirchner, Emil, and James Sperling
    1996   *Recasting the European Order* (Manchester: Manchester University Press).
Koskenniemi, Martti
    1998   *International Law Aspects of the European Union* (The Hague: Kluwer Law International).
Krenzler, Horst G., and Henning C. Schneider
    1994   'Die Gemeinsame Aussen- und Sicherheits-politik der Europäischen Union - Zur Frage der Kohärenz', *Europarecht Heft* 2: 62-78.
La Serre, Françoise de, and Helen Wallace
    1997   *Les coopérations renforcées: une fausse bonne idée?* (Paris Publication; Paris: Notre Europe).
Lenzi, Guido
    1997   'European Security after Amsterdam', CFSP Forum, Bonn, No. 3.
Libal, Michael
    1997   *Limits of Persuasion Germany and the Yugoslav Crisis, 1991–1992* (London: Praeger).
Lister, Marjorie
    1997   *The European Union and the South* (London: Routledge).
Lodge, Juliet, and Val Flynn
    1998   'The CFSP after Amsterdam: The Policy Planning and Early Warning Unit', *International Relations* 14, April.
Martin, Laurence, and John Roper
    1995   *Towards a Common Defence Policy* (Paris: Institute for Security Studies).
Mayne, Richard
    1969   *The Recovery of Europe* (London: Macmillan).
McGoldrick, Dominic
    1997   *The International Relations Law of the European Union* (London Longman).
Monar, Jörg
    1997   'The European Union's Foreign Affairs System after the Treaty of Amsterdam: A Strengthened Capacity for External Action', *European Foreign Affairs Review*, February.
Moreau Defarges, Philippe
    1997   'De la politique étrangère et de sécurité commune', *Défense Nationale* 4: 33-45.
Münch, Lars
    1997   'Die Gemeinsame Außen- und Sicherheitspolitik (GASP). Ein Schaf im Wolfspelz?', *Zeitschrift für öffentliches Recht* 1: 17-31.
Murphy, Daniel
    1998   'The EU's CFSP: It Is not Far from Maastricht to Amsterdam', *Vanderbildt Journal of Transnational Law* 31.4: 872-912.
Neuhold, Hanspeter
    1997   'Optionen österreichischer Sicherheitspolitik', *Österreichische Militärische Zeitschrift* 2: 36-49.

Neuwahl, Nanette
    1998   'A Partner with a Troubled Personality: EU Treaty-Making in Matters of
                CFSP and JHA after Amsterdam', *European Foreign Affairs Review.*
Neville-Jones, Pauline
    1997   'Dayton, IFOR and Alliance Relations in Bosnia', *Survival* 38.4.
Nuttall, Simon
    1992   *European Political Co-operation* (Oxford: Clarendon Press).
Owen, David
    1995   *Balkan Odyssey* (London: Victor Gollancz).
Pappas, Spyros, and Sophie Vanhoonacker
    1996   *The European Union's Common Foreign and Security Policy* (Maastricht:
                European Institute of Public Administration).
Park, William, and Gwyn Wyn Rees,
    1998   *Rethinking Security in Post-Cold War Europe* (London: Longman).
Petersen, John, and Helene Sjursen (eds.)
    1998   *A Common Foreign Policy for Europe? Competing Visions of the CFSP*
                (London: Routledge).
Piening, Christopher
    1997   *Global Europe: The EU in World Affairs* (Boulder, CO: Lynne Rienner).
Pijpers, Alfred, Elfriede Regelsberger and Wolfgang Wessels (eds.)
    1988   *European Political Cooperation in the 1980s* (Dordrecht: Martinus
                Nijhoff Publishers).
Regelsberger, Elfriede, and Wolfgang Wessels
    1998   'The CFSP Institutions and Procedures', *European Foreign Affairs
                Review.*
Regelsberger, Elfriede, Philippe de Schoutheete de Tervarent and Wolfgang Wessels (eds.)
    1997   *Foreign Policy of the European Union: From EPC to CFSP and Beyond*
                (London: Lynne Rienner).
Remacle, Eric
    1997   'Quelles évolutions pour la politique de sécurité commune?', *Damocles* 3:
                26-42.
Rhein, Eberhard
    1998   'The European Union on its Way Towards a World Power', *European
                Foreign Affairs Review.*
Rhodes, Carolyn (ed.)
    1998   *The European Union in the World Community* (Boulder: Lynne Rienner).
Rocard, Michel
    1998   'The Cost of Conflict to the EU', *European Foreign Affairs Review.*
Rosecrance, Richard N.
    1997   *Paradoxes of European Foreign Policy: The European Union. A New
                Type of International Actor* (Florence: European University Institute).
Rummel, Reinhardt
    1990   *The Evolution of an International Actor* (Boulder: Westview).
Schake, K., A. Bloch-Laine and C. Grant
    1999   'Building a European Defence Capability', *Survival*, 41.1.
Schmalz, Uwe
    1998   'The Amsterdam Provisions on External Coherence: Bridging the Union's
                Foreign Policy Dualism?', *European Foreign Affairs Review* March.

Schmidt, Peter
    1996   'German Security Policy in the Framework of the EU, WEU and NATO',
                Aussenpolitik 1: 16-27.

Seidelmann, Raimund
    1998   'Amsterdam and European Security. Lost or New Opportunity?', *La*
                nuova Unione Europea 1: 36-48.

Semrau, Stephan
    1998   *Die gemeinsame Außen- und Sicherheitspolitik der Europäischen Union*
                (Frankfurt: Lang).

Silber, Laura
    1996   *Yugoslavia: Death of a Nation* (Harmondsworth: Penguin Books).

Smith, Karen Elizabeth
    1998   *The Making of EU Foreign Policy: The Case of Eastern Europe* (New
                York: St Martin's Press).

Smith, Michael
    1994   'The European Union, Foreign Economic Policy and the Changing World
                Arena', *Journal of European Public Policy*, 1.2.

Spence, Arnhild
    1994   *Enlargement of the Union: A Step towards a Common Foreign and*
                Security Policy (Norwegian Institute of International Affairs Report, No.
                182).

Spence, David
    1999   'Foreign Ministries in National and European Context', in Brian Hocking
                (ed.), *Foreign Ministries: Change and Adaptation* (London: Macmillan):
                247-66.

Sperling, James, and Emil Kirchner
    1997a   'The Security Architectures and Institutional Futures of Post-1989
                Europe', *Journal of European Public Policy* 4.2: 155-70.
    1997b   *Recasting the European Order* (Manchester: Manchester University
                Press).

Télo, Mario
    1998   *Régionalisation et globalisation: L'Union européenne acteur interna-*
                tional dans le monde de l'après-guerre froide (De Maastricht à
                Amsterdam, Complexe, Bruxelles).

Tietje, Christian
    1997   'The Concept of Coherence in the Treaty on European Union and the
                Common Foreign and Security Policy', *European Foreign Affairs*
                Review.

Tsakoloyannis, P., and D. Bourantonis
    1998   'EU Representation in the UN Security Council', *European Foreign*
                Affairs Review.

Van Eekelen, Willem
    1998   *Debating European Security: 1948–1998* (Brussels: Centre for European
                Policy Studies).

Waever, Ole, Barry Buzan, Horten Kelstrup and Pierre Lemaitre
    1993   *Identity, Migration and the New Security Agenda in Europe* (London:
                Pinter).

Weidenfeld, Werner, and Josef Janning
    1993   *Europe in Global Change* (Gütersloh: Bertelsmann).
Whitman, Richard G.
    1998a   *From Civilian Power to Superpower?: The International Identity of the European Union* (London: Macmillan).
    1998b   'Creating a Foreign Policy for Europe: Implementing the Common Foreign and Security Policy from Maastricht to Amsterdam', *Australian Journal of International Affairs* 52.2: 165-84.
    1999   *Amsterdam's Unfinished Business? The Blair Government's Initiative and the Future of the WEU* (Paris, Institute for Security Studies, Occasional Paper).
Wylic, James
    1997   *European Security* (London: Longman).
Wyn Rees, G.
    1996   'Constructing a European Defence Identity: The Perspectives of Britain, France and Germany', *European Foreign Affairs Review* 2: 231-46.
Zielonka, Jan (ed.)
    1998   *Paradoxes of European Foreign Policy* (The Hague: Kluwer Law International).

Reports

Clément, Sophia
    1997   *La prévention des conflits dans les Balkans: Le Kosovo et l'ARY de Macédonie RIS* (Institute for Security Studies; Chaillot Papers, 30).
Cottey, Andrew
    1998   *The European Union and Conflict Prevention: The Role of the High Representative and the Policy Planning and Early Warning Unit* (International Alert Report).
Dolan, Andrew
    1997   *The European Union's Common Foreign and Security Policy: The Planning Dimension* (Brussels, ISIS, Briefing Paper 14).
Durand, Marie-Françoise, and Alvaro de Vasconcelos
    1998   *La PESC: Ouvrir l'Europe au monde* (Paris: Presses de la Fondation nationale des sciences politiques).
European Commission
    1998   *Common Foreign and Security Policy* (Bulletin of the European Union, No. 3; Office for Official Publications of the EC, Luxembourg).
Fontagné, Lionel
    1997   *The EU and the Maghreb* (Paris: Development Centre of the Organisation for Economic Co-operation and Development).
Grant, Charles
    1998a   *Can Britain Lead in Europe?* (London: Centre for European Reform).
    1988b   *Strength in Numbers: Europe's Foreign and Defence Policy* (London: Centre for European Reform).
    1999   *European Defence Post Kosovo* (London: Centre for European Reform).

Jopp, Mathias, Elfriede Regelsberger and Maximlian Schröder
   CFSP Forum (Bonn: Institut für Europäische Politik).

Lenzi, Guido (ed.)
  1988 *WEU at 50* (Paris: Institute for Security Studies).

Missiroli, Antonio (ed.)
  1999 *Flexibility and Enhanced Co-operation in European Security Matters: Assets or Liabilities?* (Paris: Institute for Security Studies, Occasional Paper, No. 6, January 1999).

Politi, Alessandro
  1997 *European Security: The New Transnational Risks* (Institute for Security Studies; Chaillot Papers, 29).

René, Leray
  1997 *La politique extérieure de sécurité de l'Europe à l'horizon 2000: Appréciation sur le Traité d'Amsterdam: Groupe d'Experts à haut niveau sur la PESC* (3rd Report, European Commission, October 1997).

Research Group on European Affairs
  1997 University Munich, Bertelsmann Science Foundation and DG 1A, European Commission, *CFSP Reform Debate and the Intergovernmental Conference? National Interest and Policy Preferences*, March 1997.

Spencer, Tom
  1999 *Report on the Role of the Union in the World: Implementation of the Common Foreign and Security Policy for 1998* (Luxembourg: European Parliament).

Tindemans, Leo
  1997 *Report on the Gradual Establishment of a Common Defence Policy for the European Union/EU, European Parliament, Committee on Foreign Affairs, Security and Defence Policy* (Luxembourg: European Parliament).

Websites

Ministry of Foreign Affairs

Austria	http://www.bmaa.gv.at/
Belgium	http///belgium.fgov.be/
Denmark	http://www.um.dk/
Finland	http://www.vn.fi/
France	http://www.france.diplomatie.fr/
Germany	http://www.auswaertiges-amt.de/
Greece	http://www.mfa.gr/
Ireland	http://www.irlgov.ie/iveagh/
Italy	http://www.esteri.it/
Luxembourg	http://www.uepres.etat.lu/
Netherlands	http://www.bz.minbuza.nl/
Portugal	http://www.min-nestrangeiros.pt/mne/
Spain	http://www.la-moncloa.es/
Sweden	http://www.ud.se/
United Kingdom	http://www.fco.gov.uk/

International Organizations

European Union	http://www.eu.int
Council	http://ue.eu.int/
European Parliament	http://www.europarl.eu.int/
Commission Directorate General IA	http://europa.eu.int/comm/dg1a/index.htm
EU-CFSP	http://europa.eu.int/pol/cfsp/index_en.htm
NATO	http://www.nato.int
United Nations	http://www.un.org
Western European Union	http://www.weu.int
OSCE	http://www.osec.org
Black Sea Economic Co-operation	http://www.iews.org/srd/bsec.nsf
Central European Initiative	http://www.digit.it/ceinet/homepag3.htm
Council of the Baltic Sea States	http://www.um.dk/english/udenrigspolitik/cbss

Miscellaneous

Institute for Foreign Policy Analysis	http://www.ifpa.org/ifpa_start.htm
Danish Institute of International Affairs	http://www.dupi.dk/
European Commission Task Force for Accession Negotiation	http://europa.eu.int/comm/tfan
International Alert	http://www.international-alert.org/
International Crisis Group	http://www.intl-crisis-group.org/icccghome.htm
Institute of International Affairs (Rome)	http://ww4.iol.it/iai/
Netherlands Institute of International relations 'Clingendael'	http://www.clingendael.nl/
Stockholm International Peace Research Institute	http://www.sipri.se
Norwegian Institute of International Affairs	http://www.nupi.no
Hellenic Foundation for European and Foreign Policy	http://www.eliamep.gr/
Centre for Defence Studies; King's College	http://www.kcl.ac.uk/depsta/rel/cds
Centre for European Reform	http://www.cer.org.uk/wg_ir_3.htm
Centre for European Policy Studies	http://www.ceps.be
European Foreign Policy Bulletin	http://www.iue.it/EFBB/welcome.html
General information	http://www.adminet.com/world/gov/

General Index

Name Index

UNIVERSITY ASSOCIATION FOR CONTEMPORARY EUROPEAN STUDIES
UACES Secretariat, King's College London, Strand, London WC2R 2LS
Tel: 020 7240 0206 Fax: 020 7836 2350 E-mail: admin@uaces.org
http://www.uaces.org

UACES

University Association for Contemporary European Studies

The Association
- Brings together academics involved in researching Europe with representatives of government, industry and the media who are active in European affairs
- Primary organisation for British academics researching the European Union
- Over 500 individual and corporate members from Dept such as Politics, Law, Economics & European Studies, plus a growing number of Graduate Students who join as Associate Members

Membership Benefits
- Individual Members eligible for special highly reduced fee for The Journal of Common Market Studies
- Regular Newsletter - events and developments of relevance to members
- Conferences - variety of themes, modestly priced, further reductions for members
- Publications, including the new series *Contemporary European Studies*, launched in 1998
- Research Network, and research conference
- Through the European Community Studies Association (ECSA), access to a larger world wide network
- Information Documentation & Resources eg: The Register of Courses in European Studies and the Register of Research into European Integration

Current Cost of Membership per annum - Individual Members - £20.00; Graduate Students £10.00;
Corporate Members £40.00 (2 copies of documentation sent and any 2 members of Dept / Organisation eligible to attend conferences at Members' rate)

APPLICATION FOR MEMBERSHIP OF UACES

Please indicate if you wish to receive details of the JCMS ☐

I enclose Banker's Order / cheque for £ _____ payable to UACES

Name Prof/Mr/Dr/Ms _____

Faculty / Dept _____

Institution _____

Address _____

_____

Tel No: _____

Fax No: _____

E-mail: _____

Signature & Date _____

Address for correspondence if different:

_____

_____

Where did you hear about UACES? _____

_____

BANKER'S ORDER FORM (UK Bank only)

Please return ORIGINAL to UACES and not to your Bank

TO_____(Bank)

_____(Sort Code)

AT _____(Address)

_____

Please pay to Lloyds Bank (30-00-08), Pall Mall Branch, 3-10 Waterloo Place London SW1Y 4BE

in favour of UACES Account No 3781242

on the _____day of _____

the sum of £20 (TWENTY POUNDS) and the same sum on the same date each year until countermanded

Signature & Date _____ _____

Account No _____

Name _____

Address _____

_____